Brigade Cor.
Afghanistan

PORTRAIT OF HENRY BROOKE

Brigade Commander: Afghanistan

The Journal of the Commander
of the 2nd Infantry Brigade,
Kandahar Field Force
During the Second Afghan War

Henry Brooke

LEONAUR

Brigade Commander: Afghanistan
by Henry Brooke

First published under the title
Private Journal of Henry Brooke

Leonaur is an imprint
of Oakpast Ltd

Copyright in this form © 2008 Oakpast Ltd

ISBN: 978-1-84677-570-3 (hardcover)
ISBN: 978-1-84677-569-7 (softcover)

http://www.leonaur.com

Publisher's Notes

Contents

Preface

The following *Journal* or *Diary* was written by my dear husband—to use his own words—"for you, of course, first, but
written in this form specially for the dear chicks, and therefore
quite simple and plain, so as to interest and amuse them; but I
shall be very glad if it interests the others if you will send it the
rounds, as then I need not try to write the same story over and
over again, which is very tiresome."

When on the 20th March, 1880, being at the time adjutant-
general of the Bombay army, my dear husband, to his infinite
satisfaction and delight, and full of ardour and zeal, was ordered
to the front, to take command, as brigadier-general, of the 2nd
Infantry Brigade at Kandahar, Southern Afghanistan; knowing
how deeply interested we (his wife, and children, his mother,
brothers and sisters) would be in all his movements and actions,
he conceived the idea of writing this *Journal*, and most regularly
week by week, as he found time to write, and as the Indian
mail arrived, did I receive it, and most eagerly was it looked
for and read. It will be seen that at first going off the wording
of it was simple so that the children might easily understand
all that their dear father was doing, and small details describing
the various stages of his journey up to Kandahar from Bombay
are fully entered into with the object of amusing and interesting them, and that they might the more readily picture him
both then, and when later on, having reached Kandahar, and
before troubles began, he amused himself by daily rides into the

neighbouring fields and orchards, and still further into the villages and surrounding districts, not always unattended without a certain amount of risk and danger, and thus became acquainted intimately with the country within twelve or fifteen miles of Kandahar.

But as difficulties developed themselves, and were followed, first by the lamentable defeat and retreat from the battlefield of Maiwand, of a portion of the already too small force that was holding, what appeared to him, the very false military position at Kandahar, and ended as a climax, in the Siege of Kandahar itself, the subject matter of the Journal necessarily became of such painful interest, that the language of it on many points almost went beyond the comprehension of the children, or, at any rate, was not too "simple" for their elders, albeit only too "plain" and grievous for all to read hereafter, when we remembered that he, whom we so dearly loved, had been besieged within the walls of that city, and had been in daily danger of losing that life so valuable to his wife and children, and which, alas! it was God's will—before the Kandahar garrison was relieved—should be sacrificed in the performance, in the first instance, of his duty, as a true and ardent soldier in the service of his Queen and country, during the sortie upon the village of Deh Khoja on the 16th August, 1880, while in command of the attacking party; and, more directly, in the endeavour to rescue from a cruel death a brother officer—Captain Cruikshank of the Royal Engineers—whom he found in the village severely wounded and unable to save himself!

This sortie had been determined upon six days before it was actually undertaken, and strongly then objected to, for various sound military reasons, by my dear husband, as we now know by what is written in the *Journal* of the events that daily occurred during the siege of Kandahar, and also from friends who were there themselves, extracts from whose letters—giving us the sad details of that ill-fated sortie—will be found in the Appendix. These extracts speak volumes of themselves, and need no comment from me. The manner and character of my dear husband's self-sacrificing death are indications in themselves of the ruling power which influenced all his actions.

It will be seen that the *Journal* itself ends abruptly with the events of the 14th August—all that happened afterwards we have learnt through the letters of kind friends—and when the former was written it was never intended that it should have been printed, but as all relating to my dear husband has now become of painful interest to those most nearly connected with him, I have been asked, and have yielded to the temptation, to print it as it stands, for private circulation among his nearest relations, to whom he was, in each relation of life, without reproach, and who now mourn his irreparable loss.

Annie Brooke,
Ashbrooke,
Brookeboro',
Ireland,
June 18, 1881.

Journal

Received Orders to Proceed to Kandahar.

On Saturday, the 20th March, 1880, I received the official notification that my appointment to the command of a Brigade of the Kandahar Force had been approved by the Viceroy, and I decided to leave for Kurrachee by the mail steamer of the 27th, as, although I had commenced my preparations a few days before, there was still a good deal to be done, and many things to be got to complete the small service kit which I had to take with me. The first thing to be thought of was some horses, as I had only one at the time, and as the season for purchasing horses in the Bombay market was over (the best time is November, December, and January, when the Arabs arrive from the Persian Gulf with horses), I knew there would be great difficulty in getting horses up to my weight. After many fruitless visits to the various stables, I heard of a very large and handsome Arab for sale at the stables of Addool Rahman, the great horse dealer of Bombay, who strongly recommended me to buy him if I was prepared to give the long price asked (£120).

After seeing him and riding him, I quite came to the conclusion he was worth the money, and purchased him, getting him for £110. I then bought a Persian horse out of Sir Richard Temple's stud, for which I gave £60, and with my old friend, a chestnut Australian horse which I have now had for four years, I felt quite made up, and requiring only a pony, which I will get in Beloochistan. I have named the Arab horse (an iron grey)

11

"Akhbar," the Persian (also a grey) "Selim," and the Australian's name is "Rufus." Before going further I must mention that I nearly lost both my new purchases the day after they came into my stables, as the Arab got a bad attack of colic, and the Persian got away from the man who was leading him, and got a very bad cut on his hind leg from some wire paling, but fortunately both got better much more quickly than I hoped, and seem very happy and comfortable in their stalls on board this ship today (S.S. *Umballa*, at sea March 28th).

The next thing to do was to find servants, and in this I think I have been fortunate, having got a quiet Portuguese as general servant, to take care of my clothes, cook, and make himself generally useful. He is to get 25 *rupees* a month, his clothes and food. Each horse has its groom, and they seem good sort of men, but there is not much choice, as one has to take pretty much what can be got, as there is not much desire among this class of men to see foreign parts. They each get 15 *rupees* a month, and their clothes and food. After the horses and servants were procured the next consideration was how to get all the things I wanted to take with me into the limit of weight allowed us by the regulations. I have, of course, considerably more than other officers, but even so I find it quite impossible to manage all I should like to do, so I have brought about 100 lbs. over, my weight, as I can easily take any quantity I like as far as the railway goes (*i.e.,* to Sibi), and I am told beyond that I shall perhaps be able to hire some private carriage to take the extra quantity on to Kandahar, and certainly to Quetta, where it can be left, and sent on after me to Kandahar, when the press of sending up troops is over.

Even with this extra weight I have been obliged, of course, to limit greatly my desires and wants, but I hope I have got together a fairly compact kit with nothing but what is absolutely necessary in it. First of all I have two very small trunks, which contain my clothes (all of which are uniform), shirts, &c, &c. I have, as a great treat, brought two white shirts, to be worn on high days and holidays, as a change from the coloured flannel shirts which, though useful and appropriate for the occasion, are articles of dress I dislike very much. As the cold season is now past, and it is heat rather than cold we shall suffer from, it has not been necessary to bring up warm clothing, although, of course, I have a few warm things in case of meeting sudden changes of temperature which is quite possible. General Hogg, the quartermaster-general, presented me with an excellent breech-loading revolver, and I have purchased a sword belt of the kind called the "Sam Browne Belt" (having been invented by General Sir Sam Browne), as it is so arranged that without inconvenience the pistol and ammunition can be carried on it, and the sword itself can be arranged according to one's pleasure, for riding or walking, which is a great convenience.

The Government carry for me 200 lbs. weight of tents (for other officers only 100 lbs.), so I have purchased two tents, one for myself and the other for the servants. My tent is nine feet by eight, and has a double top as a protection against the sun, and a sort of small veranda on one side, which can be used as a bath-room. The furniture of the tent consists of a bed six feet long and two feet three inches wide, a small folding table and one chair. When I get to Kandahar, if obliged to live in a tent, I will, of course, supplement this scanty supply by such articles of native manufacture as I can get. I have a block tin basin, but no tub, as that is too bulky and heavy, and the custom on the march is to have the water-carrier (*bheestie*) to empty a skin of water over one, which, though not so comfortable as a marble bath, answers all the purposes very well.

My cooking utensils are so arranged as to go into a strong basket two feet high and twelve inches in diameter. In this there are three saucepans, which fit one into the other, a kettle, a stew-pan, a frying-pan, and a pewter teapot, and two teacups and saucers pack into the saucepans, and two soup plates and two dinner plates, enamelled iron, go into the stew-pan. In my luncheon basket are three knives, three forks, three spoons, and a couple of glasses, so on a pinch I can give a dinner party of two, without resorting to the usual fashion, which is that when you are asked to dinner in camp you bring your own knives, forks, plates, glass, and generally your chair, your host supplying only the table, food, and, if he is a very good manager and very generous, drink. Of course as the country gets more opened up, native traders will push forward, and everything one can want will be procurable, although, of course, at exorbitant prices; and even now I hear almost anything can be bought at Quetta, and a good number of things at Kandahar. My establishment and kit are therefore constituted as follows:—

1 General man servant,
3 Native grooms,
3 Horses,
2 Tents,
2 Trunks,
1 Table,
1 Bed,
1 Chair,
Cooking utensils and plates, glasses, knives and forks for two.

I have brought up with me a dozen case of whiskey, and two small boxes containing a carefully selected assortment of stores to eke out the rations on the march. I have brought some soups, some chocolate and milk, biscuits, sardines, macaroni, tea, pickles and sauces. How far I shall be able to get these three little boxes I don't know, but at the worst they can easily be got to Quetta, and after that must follow me as they can. On the whole, I am quite satisfied with all my arrangements, especially with my horses, which, if I can only land them safely at Kurrachee (a very troublesome business) and get them to the end of the railway journey without hurt, will, I think, turn out well, and I am sure I hope so, as all one's efficiency and usefulness (to say nothing of one's comfort and safety) depends on being well mounted, and being able to move about rapidly and see everything for oneself. My saddles (each horse has his own) are all fitted with arrangements for carrying coats, rugs, &c, &c, and extras of all sorts, and during the march the horses I am not riding will have to carry their own clothing, and also that of the horse I ride and of the *syces* (native grooms).

It will be quite a delightful change to me, after eight years continuous office work day after day from ten till five, to live an active life constantly in the saddle and knocking about, and I feel sure the change will be very good for me in every way. I have brought with me a Persian Grammar and Dictionary, and intend, when settled at Kandahar, to work up a little Persian which might prove useful to me some day or other. The last week at Bombay was very busy, as, in addition to my preparation for a start, I wanted to keep up my work to the last, and leave nothing unfinished, which I am glad to think I did. I had farewell dinners to go to every night, and indeed had not nights enough nearly to enable me to accept all the invitations I received. I must not forget to say that among other superfluities which I have left behind me at Bombay, are my razors and shaving brush, as I don't intend to use either till I return to civilization. To-day is the second day without shaving, and I am very glad to feel that I have only men in the same stage as myself to meet, as one feels very dirty and scrubby, and will continue to do so for the next month at least, especially as I have had my hair and whiskers very well cropped, which, if not becoming, is certainly very convenient.

On Saturday, the 27th, at 6 o'clock, I went down to the dock to see my precious horses embarked, and found Alfred Christopher had arrived before me and was superintending their embarkation, which we managed without any difficulty, and then drove back to the camp, where we breakfasted with Colonel and Mrs. Wardrop, and at 10 a.m. embarked in the steamer *Umballa* for Kurrachee. At the embarking place several of my friends had come to see me off, and General Aitchison, Colonel Maude, and Colonel Wardrop came off to the ship with me and remained until we were going to sail. On board, besides myself, there is Colonel Anderson, who commands one of the Native Infantry Regiments at Kandahar, returning from sick leave in England; Captain Cooke-Collis, who is going up as brigade major of one of the Infantry Brigades; and a young gunner called Fox going to join his battery at Kandahar.

We can just make up a quiet rubber at whist, which is an advantage, as if we can we intend to travel together all the way. There are only two steamers in the week from Bombay to Kurrachee—one on Tuesday which goes direct to Kurrachee in sixty hours (the distance being under 600 miles), and the one leaving on Saturday which calls in at four ports on the way, and takes seventy-two hours. We shall, therefore, not be at Kurrachee till Tuesday in the forenoon, not in time, I fear, to get off by that evening's train for Sibi. I was rather afraid we were going to have bad weather, but it was very fairly smooth for the first twelve hours after leaving Bombay, but early this morning, Sunday, 28th March, the wind freshened a good deal, and I found it difficult to get through my dressing, and considered it advisable not to attempt to come down to breakfast, but to satisfy myself with a frugal meal of toast and iced water on deck. We have just been into the little Port of Verawul where we dropped our mails and some passengers (natives), and are now on our way to another small place (Porebunder) where we shall be in an hour or so.

The sea is calmer again, I am glad to say, so I have been able to manage to write. We hear that the heat in Sind, and until one gets into the highlands near Quetta, is very great, or, at least, was so by the latest accounts, but as it is still rather early for very great heat even in those parts, I hope it may have cooled down a bit before Ave arrive. I am a little bit nervous for fear I should be stopped at Sibi to superintend the forward movement of troops from that place. General Burrows is now there, and has been there for the last six weeks, and he may have arranged to move forward on my arrival, leaving me there till all the troops are passed (about a fortnight later). I hope this will not be the case, but I shall not be surprised if it is, as he has had his share of the work there, especially as Sibi (pronounced See-bee) is, I am told, the most awful place for heat, flies, dust and wretchedness in the whole country.

March 29th.—Tolerably smooth sea, but very warm; called in at a small port called Mandavie where we dropped a number of native passengers, and took in several more. As the place is most uninteresting, and the sun was very hot, we did not attempt to land.

March 30th.—A very rough time last night and this morning, consequent on a strong head wind and confused sea, and I was very glad when we steamed into Kurrachee Harbour about 12 o'clock noon. A telegram just received says I am to go straight on to Kandahar.

Kurrachee, *March 30th*, 1880.—On arriving at Kurrachee the first object was to get the horses on shore, which was very successfully managed, and we had the satisfaction of seeing the whole lot safely landed without any ill results from the Journey, or the eighteen hours of heavy weather which they had gone through before reaching Kurrachee. Knowing that William French was busy packing for a start with us the following evening, I was anxious, if possible, to avoid giving him the trouble of putting me up, so went to the two hotels to try and get a room for the night, but, failing to get into either, I had to drive to William French's and ask shelter from him, and found him in great confusion, but he was able to give me an empty room in which I set up my camp bed, table, and chair, and made myself very comfortable. What I cared much more for than a room for myself (*viz.*, loose boxes for my horses), he was able to give me, and this allowed of the poor beasts getting a good roll and a rest after their seventy-two hours of standing on board ship, and preparatory to thirty-six very uncomfortable hours in the railway the next day. The Royal Artillery mess was close at hand, so I had everything necessary in the eating and drinking way without, trouble. Kurrachee was less hot than I expected to find it, and the night was actually cold.

Wednesday, 31st March.—The journey from Bombay to Kurrachee by sea may be looked on as the first stage on the way to Kandahar, the second being the railway journey from Kurrachee to Sibi, a distance of about 530 miles. Till quite lately only a portion of this distance could be done by rail, which last October only went to Sukkur, leaving 131 miles of desolate desert, for the most part, to be traversed on horseback. In October last it was decided to begin the railway to Kandahar, and the work was put in the hands of Sir Richard Temple (assisted of course by skilled engineers), who was told that no money or exertions were to be spared to complete the line as far as Sibi, so as to avoid the awful journey of nearly 100 miles across a sandy desert, without water and without shade.

Owing to the extraordinary energy displayed a feat was accomplished which, I believe, has never been approached; as a train drawn by an engine entered Sibi, 131 miles from the junction with the old line, in 101 days from the date on which the first sod was turned, being at the rate of one and a third miles of line each day. No one who has not had to cross the great Cutchi Desert, which lies between Jacobabad and Sibi, can, I believe, imagine what a terrible journey it was, but the number of men and animals who have died of thirst and heat in trying to cross it, proves very clearly the horrors of the journey. Now one goes through it in a comfortable first-class carriage during the night, and the discomfort and danger is a thing of the past. The train for Sibi leaves Kurrachee at 6 p.m., at which hour our party of the *Umballa*, reinforced by William French and his horse, left for the second stage of our journey. The evening and night was fairly cool, and we all slept very well all night, having passed by Hyderabad about midnight, and not waking until we were 200 miles on our way.

April 1st.—We had a very fair breakfast at one of the refreshment-rooms, and were fortunate enough to have a moderately cool day. The railway strikes the River Indus at Kotree, opposite Hyderabad, and runs parallel with the river to Sukkur, about ten miles short of which places, at a station called Ruk, we turned off on to the branch line for Sibi, which, passing through Shikarpore, reaches Jacobabad in about thirty-six miles from the junction. The whole of Sind, for want of water, is a desolate, dusty waste, with but few trees, but the whole country covered with a low underwood which would possibly be green were it not for the heavy coat of dust which is always on it. There is little or no cultivation, except where water is obtainable from canals or wells, and consequently there are but few houses or villages, and one may go for miles without seeing a living creature.

Even birds seem to think Sind too dreadful, a place to live in. Shikarpore, which is a very large village, is a remarkable place, as poor and squalid as it looks it is inhabited by some of the richest men in India, native bankers, who trade with all parts of the world, having their correspondents in every great city in Europe, Asia, and America; and in this dirty village, in the middle of the jungles of Sind, an order for £1,000 could be obtained on London, Paris, St. Petersburg, or New York without the slightest difficulty. Shikarpore used in past days to be the great mart to which all the merchandise of Central Asia came, and from there was passed on, on the backs of camels, to Calcutta and Bombay, and from there to Europe and America. A railway to Kandahar will, of course, ruin Shikarpore, and even now it has begun to lose its importance.

Twenty-six miles beyond Shikarpore we came to Jacobabad (or the town of Jacob), so named after General Jacob, an officer of the Bombay army, who, some forty years ago, established a military station at the place which was then known Khanpur, since which time three native cavalry regiments and one native infantry regiment has always been kept at Jacobabad, as a frontier station, to keep the wild tribes which live in the surrounding hills in order. At Jacobabad we were met by the officer commanding who had prepared dinner for us, which, with a bottle of champagne, we found very refreshing, after twenty-four hours of dust and heat in the train. At half-past eight o'clock, p.m., we started again, and nine miles from Jacobabad entered on the Cutchi Desert which proved on this occasion to be singularly cool and pleasant, and we all slept with much satisfaction until half-past four, a.m., on the 2nd April (Friday) when we were woke up by the cry of "Sibi," "Sibi," to which we added "change here for Quetta and Kandahar."

It was quite cold when we arrived, and we kept under our rugs and blankets until it began to get light, when we turned out to collect our things, and get the horses disembarked. The line goes on to about eight miles from Sibi to a place called the Nari Gorge (you will see the Nari River on the map), but as this would take us several miles to the right of the direct road to Quetta, and into very wild and dangerous country, travellers are required to get out at Sibi and follow the more circuitous route by the Bolan Pass to Quetta. The first view of Sibi is not exhilarating. Sand-hills everywhere, not a blade of grass, not a tree, and not a drop of water. A few tents here and there, huge piles of bags full of grain, a string of camels, or a procession of creaking carts, drawn by two bullocks each, make up a scene which, curious by itself, is made still more odd by the sight of railway engines moving about, and all the ordinary work of a railway station going on, as it were, in the midst of a desert.

A little further on, at the back of one of the sand hills, we came to the tent of my friend General Burrows, who is commanding here, and hospitably arranged to put up William French and me, and feed us while we are here. I suppose it is hardly necessary to say that putting up in this part of the world does not mean a nicely furnished bed-room and a comfortable sitting-room, and all the luxuries of the season, but, even so, it means a good deal. First of all a tub of water and lots of soap, a cup of tea, and a right to put your camp bed either in the tent, or outside of it, according as the night proves hot or cold.

At present the heat at Sibi during the day in tents is unbearable, and so all the Europeans in the place congregate in a small three-room shed, which has been built for the purpose, and in which a rough kind of mess is kept for all comers. I am writing in this place now (as tents won't be possible till five o'clock in the evening), and writing under the circumstances is not very easy, which must be my excuse for any shortcomings in today's portion of my *journal*. On arrival here we heard that an officer had been set on by a tribe, supposed up to this time to have been friendly, and had been killed. This officer is Captain Howe Showers, who was A.D.C. to his father, General Showers, when I was A.A.G. at Calcutta, in 1865-66. It appears that he was passing through a part of the country to the right of the road from Sibi to Quetta, and thinking it quite safe had reduced his escort from fifty native cavalry (of an irregular levy he had just raised) to twelve or fifteen men.

At a spot in the hills called Chappur the party were fired on by a large party of men, who had up to that moment been concealed in the rocks. At the first volley Showers fell dead, as did also two of his men, and the remainder immediately retired, which could not be wondered at, seeing they were really no better men (probably worse) than the much stronger party who were safely posted in the rocky gorge of the mountain. We hear by telegraph from Quetta that one of the friendly native chiefs succeeded in securing poor Showers' body and those of his two men, and is bringing them into Quetta. An avenging force is today being concentrated at Chappur to punish this treacherous attack, and, I hope, will prove successful. The operations along this country are in General Burrows' hands, and he is proceeding there tomorrow, and as he is receiving good reinforcements from India, I have no doubt he will quickly mete out the proper punishment to all concerned; though for my own part, had I been commanding here, I think I should not have allowed any attack to be made until I had some artillery at my disposal, and then only under my own command, or that of some selected officer.

I think the state of the tribes along these Marri Hills is such as to cause some anxiety, as though not powerful for real harm, they are sufficiently strong to be very mischievous, and by constant raids and attacks may succeed in frightening away the workmen on the line of railway now being pushed on from Nari Gorge through Hurnai to Gwal. These places will be seen on the map, as also a place called Thai, or Tull which is one of the positions which we hold in some strength. I may as well mention that a very strong difference of opinion exists among people who are in a position to judge as to the proper line for the railway to take from Sibi to Quetta—one side, led by Sir Richard Temple, have advocated the line by Nari (I see these places are not marked on my map, but a place called Baghao is in much the same line), Harnai, and Gwal, in preference to the one through the Bolan Pass. The former is shorter and easier in an engineering point of view, but it is through a country which, if not actually hostile, which many say it is, is certainly unfriendly

The latter, on the contrary, has many engineering difficulties, but is through a comparatively safe country. The advocates of the former route have carried the day, and I fear poor Showers' death goes some way to prove that those who thought the other route would be the best in the end were not very far wrong. I am now sorry that I am not to take General Burrows' place here, as I think there will be a good deal to interest one in these parts for some time. We have settled to march very early tomorrow morning, and hope to get away from this so as to be on our new ground and tents pitched before the sun can make itself felt. The first four days after leaving Sibi will be hot, but after that we shall get into a more reasonable temperature. Our route from here lies through Kirta, Beebee-Nani, and Sir-i-Bolan, all of which are shown on the map I sent two mails ago. (The figures on that map, under the names of places, show their heights above the sea level in feet).

Friday, 2nd April.—At Sibi there are enormous depots of all sorts of commissariat stores, provisions, and clothing, both for native and English troops, all of which have had to be transported great distances, especially the grain and the clothing, as most of the former comes from Bengal, and nearly all the latter from England, or at nearest from Bombay. Thousands of pounds of grain is daily used to feed the transport animals who are in thousands—camels, horses, bullocks (both for carts and packs), ponies and donkeys. Besides these there are some 2,500 to 3,000 cavalry and artillery horses, and about 1,000 horses, the property of officers, to be fed every day, and as there is little or no cultivation in Afghanistan, some idea may be formed of the arrangements, the labour, and the expense which are required to keep this one matter of the forage supply in working order.

Armies fighting in Europe can expect to draw a good proportion of their supplies from the country in which they are operating, but the fact that almost nothing required by European troops, and very few of the articles required by native soldiers are to be got in Afghanistan, renders a war such as that we are now engaged in, a fearfully difficult and expensive matter. We dined at the rough camp mess at Sibi at which fifteen officers were present, and went to bed (in the open air) at 9 p.m., as we had to be up at 1 o'clock to pack our camels for a start at 2 a.m., as we proposed to march fourteen miles to Muskaff.

Saturday, 3rd April.—I was woke at 1 o'clock, and after dressing almost in the dark began to have the camels loaded, but everything was against us. First of all, for the six camels sent for mine and William French's baggage, only one camel driver appeared, and he seemed perfectly ignorant of everything connected with camels, and more especially with that most delicate of arrangements, the loading of a camel; and to make matters worse he proved to be a wild villager from the neighbouring hills, whose language we could not understand, nor could he understand us. Then nearly all the ropes and harness required for the pack saddles were wanting, and the saddles themselves were of the most antiquated patterns.

After many delays these minor difficulties were partially overcome, and after at least an hour spent in vain attempts to load the six camels, we had the proud satisfaction of seeing two of the lot ready for a start, when a demon entered into the two loaded animals, who rose from the ground (camels sit down to be loaded) and kicked the whole of their loads off. In the first instance this was rather ludicrous, and we laughed at it, and began again; but when 4 o'clock came, and daylight (which meant intense heat) began to appear, and yet not one camel could be induced to let the loads remain on their backs, things looked serious, and we despaired of getting off at all. However, we determined to make one final effort, and this time were so far successful that we made a start at 5 a.m., meeting the rest of our party about a mile out of Sibi, and heard to our distinct satisfaction that they had been equally unfortunate, and had only succeeded in getting off after many failures. The only wonder was that we got off at all, as it turned out that the camels had only been purchased two or three days, and were perfectly untrained.

Our satisfaction at effecting a move was but of short duration, as we had not gone a mile before half the loads were on the ground, and had to be repacked again and again. The sun was by this time too high to allow us to think of our completing the distance originally intended, so at 8 o'clock we halted for the day on the banks of the Nari River, where there is a depot of transport animals to supply changes of bullocks for the cart train which passes daily each way between Sibi and Quetta. To carry this out there are reliefs of bullocks every six or seven miles, and the arrangement works with wonderful regularity. We could not afford time to march only six or seven miles a day, so could not avail ourselves of the cart train, but are condemned to the daily trial of loading camels, than which nothing is more trying to the temper, I am bound to say.

The transport officer at the halting place was good enough to allow us to share his hut, and so saved us going into tents in which the thermometer during the day stood at 120 degrees, and even in our kind friend's hut was over 100 degrees, a heat which is required to be felt to be understood, as the entire absence of air, except now and then a hot blast, as if out of a furnace, made it most oppressive. Towards 6 o'clock it grew wonderfully cooler, and at 6.30, when we sat down to dinner at a table placed in the open, it was quite delightful.

This was the first of our mess, and, considering we were in the wilds, we did very well, having some preserved soup, a leg of mutton, and curry of sardines—I don't, however, recommend the latter to anyone who is not very hungry and hopeless of getting anything else—whiskey and water—very little of the former, and a very bad quality of the latter—completed the sumptuous repast. Just as dinner was over a noise was heard from the line of horses to which we all rushed to find that Mr. Selim (who is a pugnacious sort of gentleman) had drawn his picket pegs and was doing his best to completely destroy poor Rufus, who being picketed was powerless to retaliate. For about ten minutes we were afraid we should lose Selim altogether, as the night was dark, and if he had rushed away into the open plain we should never have seen him again. Fortunately he was too anxious to return to finish his fight with Rufus, and we managed at last to catch him, neither horse being, wonderful to say, anything the worse.

The fact is the horses are all quite wild after their long confinement and want of work, and this is a thing three or four heavy marches will all too quickly cure. To pay him out for his games, I decided to give Selim the pleasure of carrying me the first ten miles the following morning, Akhbar bringing me in the last five miles, and so giving Rufus an off day to allow him to recover the effects of his bites. We turned into bed at 8.30, sleeping, as usual in these parts, in the open air.

April 4th.—After several false starts, and many difficulties in loading the camels, we started at 3-15 a.m. for a fifteen miles march, and as I wanted to inspect the transport and commissariat depots at Muskaff, I rode on in front with a couple of the men of my escort (I have a native officer and twenty men of one of our native cavalry regiments, the Poona Horse, as an escort to Kandahar), and having a second horse for a change half way had a very pleasant canter on Selim (the first time I had ridden him), whom I like very much indeed. The two colonels followed at a quieter pace, leaving Captain Collis and Mr. Fox to bring up the rear. It was a lovely morning, and the road was very nice for cantering, and I enjoyed the ride and the attending circumstances very much.

After inspecting at Muskaff, I got on my Arab (Akhbar) and had a good opportunity of trying his paces, which will be very good, but at present he is quite raw and untrained, and gives one plenty to do to watch his antics, which, however, are all of the purest kind of play, as, like all well-bred Arabs, he is as gentle as possible. The latter part of the march into Pir-Chokey was very dusty and extremely uninteresting, and uncommonly hot. I picked up the colonels (who had passed while I was looking at the transport and commissariat depots at Muskaff), about two miles from the end of the march, which we completed at a quarter to 8 o'clock, but it was past ten when the baggage came up, the loads having frequently been thrown by the camels during the march, so our two young friends who were in charge arrived thoroughly tired and done up.

A little tea and a rest, however, soon put them right; and when at 6 o'clock in the evening, when the sun was setting, we all got a plunge into the Bolan River, which is a clear and extremely rapid running stream, we found ourselves as fit as possible, notwithstanding that the day had been even hotter than the previous ones. Pir-Chokey is a station established by us exactly at the mouth of the Bolan (N.B.—1st syllable short; 2nd long) Pass as a resting and feeding place for the transport animals and troops proceeding up and down. The Bolan Pass is the only really practicable passage through the range of mountains which separates India from Beloochistan and Central Asia, and has been used for ages by the caravans coming to India from all parts of Asia. Until we went up by it to Kandahar in 1839, '40, '41, the road was a mere track through the bed of the river, and on that occasion we did very little to improve it, and never dreamt that forty years later we should have to make a road practicable for wheeled carriage through it; but this is what we have done, and carts now run from Sibi to Quetta and still further on the road to Kandahar. It must not be, however, supposed that the road is of the appearance or quality that people at home would call a road, as all that has been aimed at is to make a track clear from stones or serious inequalities along which carts can, go.

At Pir-Chokey are stored thousands of pounds of grain of all sorts, flour, rice, sugar, tea, potatoes, &c, &c, indeed everything required to ration both man and beast, and many extras also, as we were able to obtain from the Government stores there, on payment, such things as Ropf's concentrated soups, French preserved vegetables, &c, &c. There is a shed for the use of officers and a couple for the men, as there is at nearly all the stages in the pass, which is a very good arrangement, as it saves us pitching tents, and the huts are much cooler than tents during the day; and as dew or damp are unknown here everyone sleeps in the open at night. We were in bed at half-past 8, and I was so dead tired that I never woke through all the row of the packing, but had the satisfaction when I woke to find the camels gone and everything packed. Captain Collis, my brigade major, is very good in this way, and does a great deal for me, which my orderly officer would have to do if I had one, and as I might have had, had General Warre been agreeable and allowed me to take the officer I wanted.

April 5th.—As we had a very long march (between nineteen and twenty-one miles) we had to move off very early, the more especially as I had two sets of depots to inspect on the way; we had let the baggage have three hours start of us, having sent the native officer and sixteen men with it, keeping only four men for ourselves, as we considered our five selves good for any number of the cowardly marauders who hang about the pass, but who never seem to venture to attack armed parties, but always to swoop down on one or two unarmed natives if they get the chance. 500 yards out of Pir-Chokey we had to ford the Bolan River, and the winding course it takes may be imagined from the fact that in the first ten miles of the march we forded it eighteen times. It is, however, never more than a couple of feet deep, and from ten to fifty yards wide.

The whole of the road from Pir-Chokey to Dirwaza (seventy-eight miles) is called the Bolan Pass, and most of the way is properly so called, though there is a great plain of twenty miles across, which, though surrounded in the distance by hills, has none of the appearance of what one understands as a pass. For the first twelve miles the road is indeed a pass or gorge in the mountains, as in places the cliffs are not more than 60 to 100 yards apart, and rarely open out to more than 150 to 200 yards apart. Passing along this in the early morning with the moon just setting is very striking and dismal, as the hills, which are very peculiarly shaped, are very high and abrupt, and are absolutely bare of vegetation of any kind, except that the banks of the river are here and there fringed with Pampas grass and Oleanders, the latter just now in full blow, and very sweet. It is quite the most desolate, forsaken scene I have ever witnessed, and the least enlivening.

It is fortunate that the tribes in the vicinity of the Bolan Pass are fonder of *rupees* than of fighting, as they could easily prevent anyone passing up if they so desired it, but for a consideration (a very heavy subsidy, I fancy) they agree not only not to resist our advance, but to act as the police of the pass, and so enable us to dispense with any great strength of soldiers here.—I must digress for one moment to describe the circumstances under which I write, so that allowances may be made for bad writing and stupidity. First of all, I am in a large tent, permanently pitched, as there is no rest hut here (Beebee-Nani, April 6th), the thermometer is at 96°, a gale of wind is howling outside, and shaking the tent so violently that I watch the poles with apprehension; everything is gritty with the clouds of dust that are flying about; the flies, which are in millions, I should say, are gifted with a pertinacity which is quite marvellous, and insist on settling on your nose, or in your eyes or ears; my four companions are stretched on the ground fast asleep (I never sleep myself in the day time), and by some curious fatality have, one and all, established themselves on their backs, and are snoring most awfully; and last, but not least, the heat is making the ink quite thick and preventing it running freely, and with it my ideas also I fear. I think it will be acknowledged that any one or two of these drawbacks would be fair excuses for not doing much writing, so I hope the lot together. will bear me harmless from criticism now and hereafter.—To return to my story now:

As the sun began to rise the whole scene changed, and what had seemed weird and desolate now got a colour that made the scene one that I would not have missed for any consideration; the effect altogether, of course, of the beautiful colouring which sunrise always bring with it in the East, but which rapidly fades as the sun gets higher. At nine miles from Pir-Chokey I came to one of the transport stages, which I found in charge of a sergeant of the 66th Foot, with a guard of twelve native soldiers; not another European within ten miles of him on either side. He said it was, of course, lonely, but he had lots to do, and that all his spare time was given to fishing in the Bolan River, which swarms with fish of the most confiding nature, as they greedily seize any sort of bait, and can even be caught in the hand at night by the use of a light—a way of catching fish not quite unknown in our own part of the world.

Five miles further on I inspected another depot, which is situated at the end of the first part of the enclosed portion of the pass, after which we descended into the plain or valley of Kirta, an extensive plain more than twenty miles across, and almost circular in shape, the mountains rising to a considerable height all round it. About six miles further ride brought us to the rest house of Kirta, where we were to put up for the day, and where, on arriving, I received the agreeable information that the camel carrying my two small trunks, which contain every stitch of uniform, clothing, linen, towels, sheets, socks, warm clothing, &c., &c, in fact, everything I possess, except what was on my back, had fallen down in one of the fords, and that the two portmanteaus had been well under water for five minutes at least.

The first and only thing to do was to open the boxes and dry the things (for which purpose there was no lack of sun, at any rate), and ascertain the amount of the damage done. Every single thing was more or less wet, but fortunately, except my cloth uniform, my few books, and my stock of writing paper, there was little to spoil seriously; my patrol jacket had got off wonderfully, having been well in the centre of one box, and was only damp, and my other cloth things had not much suffered, and the rest of the things (except my paper, books, and papers, which are ruined) will, I daresay, be all right after they have been washed and done up.

On the whole, I got off wonderfully well, but it was a great business unpacking everything, drying them, and then repacking all again, which, however, I managed to do in a fairly satisfactory way. At Kirta is another large depot for the transport and commissariat departments, and also a rather superior kind of hut for the accommodation of passersby. The plain of Kirta itself is one vast scene of desolation, not a tree, or a blade of grass, and nothing but fine sand, thickly strewn with round stones of all sizes and forms.

Monday, 5th April, continued—At the Kirta rest-house we found a very scientific party of engineers (Mr. Molesworth, Colonel Lindsay, and Major Peters), who had been prospecting the railway line to Kandahar, and were returning by no means impressed with the delights, use, or value of Afghanistan. I don't wish to form too hasty a judgement, but I must say as far as I have gone I have seen no reason to modify the opinions formed eighteen months ago, namely, that a more useless and unnecessary thing than an expedition into this country could not be imagined. Committed to it as we now are, a sudden withdrawal would be madness, and in any case, it would be a wise man who could form an idea as to the final results, or what and when the end will be.

Up to the present, though the days have been intensely hot, the nights have been very pleasant, and the mornings charming, but at Kirta just as we were looking for the change from the heat of the day to come (half-past five o'clock), the wind suddenly chopped right round and blew a hurricane, like a red-hot blast of a furnace, bringing with it thick clouds of dust, which made breathing, or keeping one's eyes open almost an impossibility. Of course I have been in many dust storms in all parts of India, but it has never been my fortune to spend so entirely miserable a time as we had to undergo between 5.30 on Tuesday evening, and 8 o'clock the next morning. The rest-house has no glass in the windows, and even had it been possible to close the wooden shutters, they were so roughly made that they would have been useless to keep out either the burning wind or 'the dust; but even the wind and dust were preferable to the suffocation of no air at all, and so, through a very long dark night, we could do nothing but toss about on our beds and long for morning.

Tuesday, April 6th.—About 3 a.m. the hurricane seemed to moderate, so we got up and dressed and set to work to pack our camels, in the middle of which operation the gale recommenced with greater force than ever, and made our work almost impossible; however, by 4 o'clock, with the assistance of some men from the transport depot the work was finished and the camels with their escort started for a nine mile march in the teeth of the gale and dust. I waited on in the rest-house till 6 o'clock in hopes of the weather changing when the sun rose, but finding no change likely, had also to face the dust and wind, and continued to ride against it for about two hours, when, getting under the shadow of a big mountain, we ceased to get the dust and the gale grew much cooler, and to our great relief we found a much more bearable climate at our halting place, a little transport depot called Beebee-Nani, where I am now writing. It cannot be called pleasant here, but compared with the past eighteen hours the change is distinctly for the better.

Desolation reigns here also, no trees or vegetation to be seen; nothing but sand, stones, and barren rocky hills rising in tiers one behind the other, till the last and highest range is barely visible in the hot and dusty haze. At this halting place there is no rest-house, but instead a good-sized tent, which answers the purpose very well. A stream of beautiful clear water flows past the tent, being brought in a small canal or channel (made by our troops) from the Bolan River, which is two miles off. The water is bright, and pure, and good, and quite cold, and is accordingly in this land of bad and scanty water a priceless luxury to all. The hill tribes near this are not very well-disposed, and they frequently cut off the water by damming up the place where it leaves the river, but a small party of native soldiers, who are at once sent out, soon hunts the enemy off, and sets the water flowing again.

We are now beginning to ascend, and it is decidedly cooler than it was (speaking comparatively), but the air is unpleasantly dry and harsh, and our lips and skin generally are suffering accordingly, all the more, no doubt, that of late we have been ac-

31

customed to the damp, relaxing climate of Bombay. This morning we passed many of the migratory tribes who, during the winter, leave the districts round Quetta on account of the cold and go with their flocks and herds down towards Sibi, where they remain till it gets too hot, when they return to Quetta. They are wretched-looking people, evidently very poor in everything except children, of whom there seems to be no lack. Their whole household goods are carried on camels, and the women and children trot along behind seemingly very happy and light-hearted.

On one camel today we saw an uncommonly pretty young donkey rolled up in a blanket with his head only to be seen, looking quite pleased with himself, and being balanced on the other side of the camel by a jolly but extremely dirty baby of eight or nine months old. They make very picturesque groups these people, but certainly among them the men carry off all the good looks, as the women seem to be singularly plain and unprepossessing. We are getting very bad hay for our horses now, which is very unfortunate, but as it has all to be brought from places miles away we ought, I suppose, to be very thankful that we get any at all. So far my three are very well, and I am quite pleased with my new purchases, and very glad, indeed, that I brought my old friend up with me, as he is a most pleasant horse to ride. To give an idea of the sort of country this is I may mention that the ground is too hard to allow of our driving in even iron picketing pegs for the horses, and we have therefore to collect a heap of heavy big stones and fasten their picketing ropes to these!

Wednesday, 7th April.—We had a very long march before us (seventeen miles) to a place called Mach (pronounced Much), so started off the heavier portion of our baggage and all our servants in charge of half of my escort at 10 o'clock the previous night,. keeping only two camels to carry our camp beds and bedding, and the warm sheets and rugs of the horses; we were to ride. We had a fairly good night's sleep, although the high wind was not pleasant, and towards morning became bitterly cold, for which some of the party were not prepared, and were consequently very cold indeed. I had my two thick blankets, and found them nothing too much, although twelve hours previously we had been undergoing a heat of nearly 100°. These changes are very trying to people who are not thoroughly strong, but barring slight colds all round, we have not suffered on this occasion.

Colonel Anderson's horse had hurt itself, so I had to give him a mount on Rufus, which, as he weighs fifteen stone and the march was seventeen miles, I would altogether have preferred not to do, but as the alternative was his walking while I had two led horses I could not possibly have done otherwise. The road for the first eight miles took us over a barren, desolate plain, across which the cold wind whistled and drove in a way that made us all wish much we had kept our great coats out, and which made us hail with delight the appearance of the sun, which up to this had been our greatest enemy. Eight miles from Beebee-Nani we came to a small transport depot called Abigoom, where I changed my horse Akhbar for Selim, who had gone on with the heavy baggage the night previously. Here Captain Collis, who had been riding some way in rear, came up to tell me that one of my *syces* (grooms) declared he was so seriously ill that he could not possibly go on, even though he knew that if left behind by himself on the side of the road he would probably be murdered by some of the ruffians who hang about to wreak their vengeance on any one who is defenceless.

Fortunately I was able to get a cart and pair of bullocks at the transport depot at Abigoom, and we went back and picked the man up and brought him into Mach, and he is all right today. I don't think there ever was much the matter with him beyond having eaten too much, which these people, now that they are fed by us and not by themselves, are very ready to do. The morning, once the sun was up, was most enjoyable, although the country we passed through was of the same desolate, dreary sort that is met in this part of the world. Brown arid mountains and red clay plains covered thickly with enormous boulders; no trees, no water (except when now and then we cross the Bolan

River), no habitations, and no cultivations.

As a sergeant of the 66th, who was in charge of one of the transport depots, said to me, "Why, sir, there are no birds in this awful country, and when I see a country as has no birds I think badly of that country." The poor fellow's views of life and of the pleasures of campaigning had been jaundiced I fancy by a lonely residence for four months in a desert without a single European near him, although he said on the whole he did not dislike it, as he had heaps to do all day, and the nights were much too short for the amount of sleep he would like to have had. Ascending gradually from Abigoom we reached an elevation of 3,500 feet at Mach, and found ourselves in an European climate, which Captain Collis and I celebrated by drinking hot whiskey punch for dinner!!

Mach is quite a big place, and there is a post office and telegraph office there, and a good rest house, and we spent a very comfortable time there, especially when we recollected the disagreeables of the previous days. We were able to replenish our larder and stores from the commissariat, getting from them bread, mutton, tea, sugar, potatoes, preserved soups, &c, &c. To my great delight I got my English letters here,— those of the 12th March, which had reached Bombay 30th March,—and we posted our letters for home, as, although it was a little too early, it was our only chance, as there is no other post office till we get to Quetta, and the English mail will have left that place before we arrive.

As the next day's march was not a long one we decided to have a good sleep, and not start till 4 a.m. (which meant getting up at 3 o'clock), and as we all turned in at half-past 8, we had had a very fair night of it, when at 3 a.m. on Thursday, April 8th, I was woke by Colonel Anderson with the extremely unpleasant news that the native officer of the escort reported that the whole of our camel drivers had disappeared—run away to their homes it was supposed. The question was what was to be done, as we had no wish to lose a day at Mach, so I sent and woke up the transport officer (a smart young fellow of the 15th Foot), who before I at all expected it, was in the rest-hut fully dressed, asking to see the "General," who being extremely cold was quite invisible among his blankets.

I had a further search then made for the camel men, but it was clear they had bolted, so I was forced very unwillingly to take advantage of my being the "General *Sahib*," and take carts to take us into Quetta. Carts are not, as a rule, given to officers, as they are used for commissariat stores, and so up to this time I have resisted the temptation of appropriating some (they are far pleasanter means of carrying baggage than camels), not wishing to have any advantages over other officers, especially at the expense of the General Transport Service; but now that the camel men had deserted I felt I might fairly take carts, as it was clearly not advantageous that I should remain idle for days at a place like Mach. I, however, kept the demands of my friends and my servants as low as possible, and we succeeded in getting off without reducing perceptibly the carrying power of the transport, or causing any stores to be delayed.

Carts drawn by bullocks are very slow, as they barely do more than If miles an hour, but they are very sure and steady, and require no elaborate packing as camels do. On the other hand they are very liable to break down or to fall over the precipices, so their possession is not an unalloyed satisfaction. On the whole I think if I had good camel men I would prefer camels. At Mach we found a Major Greig of the artillery, trying to work his way up alone, taking advantage of any convoys or escorts he could meet, and as this was very dismal and very slow, I asked him to join our party, which now numbers six. It was 5 o'clock when we succeeded in getting away from Mach, and it was then so cold that I rode the first half of the way in my great coat. The road was very up and down, and at places very steep, but still wonderfully good; the country still as barren and uninteresting as ever. Four miles from Mach we came to a place called Sir-i-Bolan, which means the head or source of the Bolan, and here are the springs from which the river rises. They rush out of the solid rock in a splendid stream, but curiously one of the jets is distinctly some degrees hotter than the others are.

Thursday, 8th April.—The place *(i.e.* Sir-i-Ab) is covered with Maidenhair Ferns, a piece of which I enclose; I have also taken a root of it, and intend to send it to Florence to see if she can force it back into life, as a plant of Maidenhair Fern from the source of the Bolan would be a kind of curiosity, I dare say.[1] After passing Sir-i-Ab, the road led through a very narrow valley, with high and precipitous cliffs on both sides, quite overhanging the road, and not more than fifty yards apart at some places. The effect is wild, and the morning air being sharp and fresh, with a bright sun, the ride was quite enjoyable.

Our halting place for the day was Dozan (or the place of thieves), which is a good sized Commissariat and Transport Station, possessing a good rest-house and quite a large number of people of sorts. There is not, however, naturally any water here, but we have brought it by an aqueduct from some spring two miles off, and there is now a plentiful and excellent supply—the last really good water we shall see for some days. This station is in charge of a very nice young fellow of the 83rd, named Adye, quite a boy, but a very good style of fellow, and one who does his work well, as his bullocks, carts, and everything in his charge shows.

The life these young fellows lead does not seem very delightful, but it is wonderful how clearly one can see which are the really good officers who take interest in their work, and have no time or inclination for grumbling about themselves, and I am delighted to say the great majority are of this sort, indeed it is the exception when the reverse is the case, and as the same can truly be said of the sergeants similarly employed (all quite young men), I don't think the army is going to the dogs quite so much as dismal prophets would have us think. It is also most satisfactory to see how well our native soldiers (non-commissioned officers and men) on this detached and independent employment get on, as they develop in intelligence and readiness in a remark-

---

1. Note.—The Fern mentioned above is now in the Stove House at Narrow Water, and has grown to quite a large healthy plant.

able way, and show that what they really want (as do our English soldiers) is less nursing and coddling, and care, and being made at all times to do more for themselves than they now are.

Friday, 9th April.—After starting off our baggage we took a detour to the right to visit a plateau about 1,000 feet higher than Dozan, where, during last summer, General Phayre's brigade had been encamped, and where, thinking the place would become a permanent station, he had expended much labour and trouble in making roads and laying out the future cantonment. Now, however, the troops are withdrawn and the place is deserted. Among other things which had been made was an excellent lawn tennis ground which looked very English and civilized in the midst of the desolation. At this place are the springs from which the halting place is supplied with water, and here, as elsewhere in this extraordinary country, it is wonderful to see the rush of water which pours out of the solid rock, reminding one (all the surrounding circumstances having also a considerable similitude) of the water rushing out of the rock when struck by Moses during the travels of the Israelites in the Wilderness.

We rejoined the road about four miles from Dozan, and for four miles our way continued through the narrowest and wildest part of the Bolan Pass, till at eight miles from Dozan we crossed an abrupt ridge of hills which lie across the mouth of the pass, and descended into a plain surrounded by mountains the tops of which were still tipped with snow. Two miles further on we came to our halting place, which is called Darwaza, or the door or gate, this being the entrance to the Bolan Pass, the journey through which we had then completed. There was a good rest-house at Darwaza, and a small fort, inside of which we were glad to find shelter for our horses and servants, as a piercingly cold wild wind was coming from the mountains, and there were decided threatenings of snow or rain, and very shortly after we arrived it did begin to rain. I had an anxious day with my Australian horse as he was very ill, and, being almost without medicines, I was afraid I should have lost him.

He had not taken at all to the bad grass or hay which we have had through the pass, and had not been really well for some days. This was what I feared in bringing him with me, as Australian horses are notoriously dainty about their food, whereas Arabs eat anything and seem to flourish on anything. We tried all the native remedies at our disposal, and the old horse pulled through all right, and before night was able to eat a bran mash and was quite out of danger. He has, however, got a cracked heel, the result of the cold dry wind after crossing the numerous fords which we have had to pass over daily, and I fear I shall not get much riding out of him, which is a disappointment, as he is a steady old boy who goes along without any trouble, while the other two are young and foolish, and as yet not contented to plod along at a walking pace for any time.

The evening at Darwaza turned out very wet and cold, and the night threatened to be so bad that we had to give up the idea of an early march which we had intended to make, so as to get over the long and wearisome journey which lay between us and our next halting place. Darwaza is one of the highest points on the road to Kandahar (the highest except the crossing of the Khojak Pass)., being 6,000 feet above the sea level, and until a month ago the whole country round had been covered with eighteen inches of snow, some of which still remained on the mountains near.

Saturday 10th April.—"We started at 6 a.m. to march to Sir-i-Ab, to reach which place we had to cross a great plain (16 miles across) which, owing to its miserable and wretchedly desolate appearance, is called the Dusht-i-bedaulat (the au has the sound of ow) or the plain of poverty or wretchedness, and certainly it well bears out its name, as for mile after mile nothing is to be seen but sand and stones, and desolation everywhere. No one lives in the place, and no one crosses it except when obliged to do so, as almost always a howling wind, which is either hot as a furnace or cold as ice, drives across it, carrying clouds of dust with it, and making the journey not only wretched but even, to weakly people and animals, dangerous.

There is no water from Darwaza to Sir-i-Ab, a very serious

consideration in the hot weather. We, however, were singularly fortunate, as the storm of the previous day had spent itself, and the rain had laid the dust, and we crossed the Dusht without the slightest inconvenience, indeed with some enjoyment, as the morning was lovely and fresh, and the mountains covered with the snow, which had fallen in the night on their higher peaks, were looking beautiful, and took away in a great degree from the otherwise desolate appearance of the scene. As we approached Sir-i-Ab, we saw more signs of civilization (though of a very rude kind) than we had met since we left Jacobabad, as there were numerous villages to be seen, each surrounded by its orchards, containing peach, plum, and mulberry trees, which were all in full leaf, and looked green and bright to us who had not seen a patch of green for so many days.

At Sir-i-Ab we put up in a deserted village, in which was established our Commissariat and Transport Depot, and a few houses which were set apart and kept clean for the use of officers and men passing through. The people to whom the village belong had migrated to the lower regions during the winter, and were now on their way back, and had sent word that after the middle of this month they would require the place for their own residence, and we were, in consequence, clearing out our Commissariat Stores and transport animals into a camp outside the village. Although the people had left the village for their own convenience, as they would have done whether we had been there or not, we had actually been paying them rent for the empty houses, and now at their request were quietly submitting to be turned out. This is the curious way we make war, and add to the terrible expenses of it quite unnecessarily. An Afghan village is a collection of mud huts, with flat mud roofs, and so arranged, and the huts joined together with high walls, as to form a kind of fort, as in this country every man's hand is against his neighbour's, and everyone goes armed and prepared for treachery and violence. The people are a distinctly warlike race, and fight bitterly among themselves.

Sunday, 11th April.—A short march of seven miles took us into

39

Quetta, which looked charming as we rode into it at 8 o'clock in the morning, the air bright and fresh, and the sun shining just sufficiently to take the sharpness out of the air. There were quantities of purple crocuses in flower, and the hawthorn was covered with flower and looked very home-like indeed. Quetta lies in a small circular plain about five miles across, surrounded by high mountains, and well watered by streams of clear water which come down from the mountains and enable the people to cultivate their orchards and fields most successfully. Originally there was only a moderately sized native town at Quetta, with, from a native point of view, a very strong fort to defend it; but since we have occupied the place (now some four years ago) houses after the English fashion have sprung up, and the place is assuming the appearance of an Indian station.

We have taken over the fort and use it as an arsenal, for which purpose it serves sufficiently well, though it would be quite use-less as a Fortification against any enemy who possessed guns of any kind. The native name of Quetta is Shawl or Shalkot, and it is by the latter name that natives generally know it. It is not in Afghanistan, but belongs to the Khan of Khelat, who has lent it or ceded it and the surrounding country temporarily to us on the understanding that we pay him as much revenue as he used to get out of it, which we find we can do, and have a good bal-ance for ourselves without oppressing the people in any way, which shows that the *khan* must have been very much cheated by his officials formerly. We have established a regular civil gov-ernment, and administer the country exactly as if it were India.

The civil authorities of course say the people like our admin-istration, but I confess I doubt it, as they are a very independ-ent lot, and prefer, I think, injustice and oppression from their own people than justice and order after an English pattern. The revenue is paid in a very primitive manner still in these parts; one-sixth of the whole produce of the land goes to the Govern-ment, and as soon as a field of wheat or an orchard of peaches is ripe, and the crop collected, Government officials go and put on one side what they consider the Government share, which is then sold by auction, the farmer taking away the remaining five-sixths; and I am told the system works well, and there is very seldom any attempts to cheat the Government of their dues.

There is a club at Quetta, of which we were made honorary members, and where we lived during our stay. The club has managed to get up a capital library, and have all the English and Indian papers and most recent telegrams, so we felt quite back in civilization again after our wanderings in the deserts and wilds of the Bolan Pass.

April 11th & 12th.—The chief civil authority at Quetta is Sir Robert Sandeman, who has an extremely nice house, very well furnished, and will eventually have very nice gardens and grounds round it. He asked me to go and put up with him, but as we had agreed not to break up our party while at Quetta, but to keep together, I refused his invitation, but dined with him one night. He is a great supporter of the policy of pushing forward our frontier into Afghanistan, and interfering in the internal arrangements of that country, and as I think we have gone much too far in that direction he and I had a good deal of warm discussion. I went with him to the hospital to see the two native soldiers who were wounded when Captain Showers was killed, and I heard from them the whole particulars of the catastrophe. It appears that poor Showers (whom I have known well for many years) was warned by some friendly native chiefs not to take the road he did, but he told them an Englishman never turned back, and he would not do so.

He had only twelve or fourteen men, all natives, with him, and at a very narrow gorge in the mountains, through which the road passed, they came upon a party of some thirty or forty men posted up among the rocks in a position quite inaccessible from the road. These men received Showers' party with a volley which killed him and a couple of his men. There was some desultory fighting between the rest of the escort and the enemy, but the unfortunate escort without their officer and down in the valley mounted could do nothing, and so the remnant had to retire, leaving three or four dead, and the two wounded men I was talking to, on the ground. The men told me that poor Showers' death must have been instantaneous, as he was hit by three bullets at the same minute, and never spoke or groaned.

Sir Robert Sandeman said to one of the men who happened to be a sergeant, that he was glad to see he was getting better, and adding "you see your fate is good"

(N.B.—This is a kind of usual expression when a person has been fortunate, as all Mohammedans are great believers in *Kismet* or fate), on which the poor fellow, with tears in his eyes and with wonderful energy and spirit, said, "Ah, *Sahib*, don't say that; don't say my fate is good, for I am filled with shame to think that my *Sahib* is dead and I am alive. It is a great shame to me that I am alive; my fate is bad." It was very touching, and there was no doubt of the man's sincerity and honesty, as we who heard him could testify to. What he said loses greatly by translation, and by not being heard, but it was really a most impressive sight.

This wild Beloochie, with his long black hair all about his face, which was quite pale from pain and loss of blood, getting, in his excitement, on his elbow as he lay in his bed and speaking with the greatest earnestness, and then falling back on his pillow quite overcome with weakness and agitation. The men all liked Showers greatly, as his pluck and dash appealed to their feelings strongly. This man was the senior of the party, and he told me he said to Showers that he had better not go by that route, but that the *sahib* only laughed and asked him if he was afraid. I asked him what he did then, and he said "Oh, the *Sahib* was only joking; he knew I was not afraid; but I wanted to save him, but of course, as he was determined to go on, we said nothing more."

When the rest of the party retired, the enemy came down and stripped the two wounded men of all their clothes, except their linen shirts and drawers, and there they lay for two nights in the piercing cold. This man said, "Oh, *Sahib*, it was so cold and I had such pain, I prayed all night to God, and said 'let me die,' but God would not let me die, and here I am. No, my fate is not good!!!"

It is a long story, but I tell it to you to show the sort of fellows many of our native soldiers are, men that anyone might be proud to serve with. For myself I would go into action with our native troops without a hesitation (especially men of certain races), assured of their fighting well and gallantly. This man of whom I have been telling you was a countryman of the people who killed Showers, and yet he was perfectly loyal, even to losing his own life, in the service he had taken. There is no doubt Showers ought not to have gone the way he did, and in no case ought he to have gone so weakly escorted. His body was recovered, and he is buried at Quetta, and punishment has been awarded to the men who attacked him.

Tuesday, April 13th.—We left Quetta on our first march out to Kandahar at quarter to six a.m., having, I am sorry to say, left behind at Quetta Captain Cooke-Collis, who was ordered by a telegram, that was awaiting him at Quetta, to remain there until the arrival of General Phayre, whose staff officer he is to be. We were very sorry to lose him, as he is a pleasant companion, active, energetic, and most obliging. I was in hopes that he was to be my Brigade Major, which he wished to be, so the arrangement now made is a disappointment to us both.

As the country between Quetta and Kandahar is more or less disturbed, and the tribes along the route are not friendly, I thought it well to increase my escort, so have added to it half a company of Infantry who will furnish sentries at night and guard the baggage on the road, while the cavalry escort will accompany me. With our five selves and half a troop of cavalry and half a company of infantry, I feel quite safe, and only fear we won't be given a chance of exchanging compliments with the tribes on our route. A wing of the 30th Native Infantry is one march ahead of us, and the 7th Fusiliers escorting £100,000 of treasure leave Quetta tomorrow, so they will be one march behind us, so we have plenty of troops on the road.

April 21st.—It is more than a week since I have been able to write up my journal, as I have, I may say, hardly been out of the saddle since the 16th, and have slept in my clothes for four nights.—*April 13th*, continued—Metarzai, the first march out from Quetta, is a wretched place, nothing but sand and Stones, no rest-house, so we had to pitch tents for the first time, and found them very hot during the daytime. The water was far from good.

April 14th.—Marched to Dina Kharez, a word which signifies "bitter waters," and most richly the place has earned its name, as more disgusting water I never tasted. Our party is a singularly temperate one, and we all prefer cold tea to any drink, but here it was quite impossible to drink the tea, as the water is quite salt, and tea made of it bore a most painful likeness to a black draught, or the senna and salts of one's youth.—By the way, why is it that the children of the present day have not to drink the great big tumblers full of senna and salts which we used to have periodically!—The road between Metarzai and Dina-Kharez (distance twelve miles) is, as usual, very uninteresting, except that it crosses what is called the Ghazerbund Pass, a moderately high range of hills; with an ascent and descent of about 700 to 800 feet. There was a rest-house at Dina-Kharez, but we all (including the horses) suffered much inconvenience for want of some decent water.

April 15th.—Marched to Segi (ten miles) the country still most uninteresting and desolate, no inhabitants and no cultivation. The heat in the daytime is very considerable, and we are all very glad when evening comes. We always dine outside in the cool, and at Segi we very nearly lost our dinner, as the soup, which is the great stand by, had just been placed on one of our rickety camp tables, when two great bull dogs who belong to members of our party, thought fit to commence a most violent fight under the tables and chairs which were scattered in all directions. Fortunately we managed to snatch the dishes off first, and so saved our dinner. I may as well here give the routine of our days, which are one just like another.

We are woke at 4 a.m., dress, pack up our beds, tents, &c, &c, put them on the carts or camels, placing materials for breakfast on a pony, as he travels much faster than camels.—March at 5 a.m., and are generally in at 8 a.m. Shortly after the pony comes up with some servants, and we have a picnic breakfast; about the time it is done the baggage comes in, and tents are pitched and boxes opened, and we dress and wash, read, write and talk till 5 o'clock, when we go out for a stroll and visit the horses, &c. Dinner at 6, and we are all fast asleep at half past 8.

Friday, 16th April.—Marched to Gulistan Kharez (ten miles) through the usual uninteresting desert, but the place itself, which literally interpreted, means "place of roses," is much better than any place we have been at yet on this side of Quetta, as there is plenty of good water (a bright flowing stream), and a few trees. Here there is in course of completion, what there ought to be at each of the stages, a small fort and enclosure for the commissariat stores. The fort would be quite sufficient to resist any attack the Afghans (without artillery) could bring against it, but to my surprise I found it had no gate or no means of closing the entrance. The engineer officer in charge of all the works on the road happened to be at Gulistan, and I sent for him and told him that I did not at all like the state of things, and that he must, at any cost, make a gate or other arrangement.

The difficulty was getting wood, of which there is none in this desolate wilderness. As a makeshift I caused the native officer in command of the post to be shown how to make a temporary barricade with carts and sand bags, and so to secure himself against a sudden rush. I dare say at the time I was thought a desperate nuisance and over particular, but if that was the idea then the next day's events quite altered their opinions.

Saturday, April 17th.—Marched to Killa Abdoola, which is eleven and a half miles from Gulistan, and five miles from the foot of the pass across the Khojak range of mountains which are there 7000 feet high. We got to the end of our march about half-past 8 o'clock, and about 10 o'clock, as we had just finished breakfast, the telegraph clerk (there is a telegraph office here) brought me an urgent message from General Phayre, who was at Chaman, on the other side of the Khojak range (sixteen miles off), to say that disturbances, the extent of which he did not yet know, had broken out between Chaman and Kandahar, and that all communication with Kandahar was closed. He asked me to come to him at once.

Our baggage animals having only just completed eleven miles, and the heat being very great, it was clear the whole party could not go on, so I decided to ride forward myself, accompanied only by one officer and five native cavalry, leaving all my baggage behind. Major Greig, of the R. A., having a fresh horse, I selected to go with me, and we started at 11.30 to ride across the Khojak to Chaman. The pass is a very narrow and difficult one, offering many opportunities for organised resistance or ambushes, but I thought on the whole it was better for me to take quite a small escort, as if the pass was held the whole of my escort could not have forced it, and if there were only a few of the enemy about we had a better chance to pass through unobserved going a small party. The proceeding was a little risky, and had it not been successful would have been disapproved, I dare say; but for myself, I confess I never expected to meet resistance, as I knew General Phayre's account of the disturbances were not at all likely to suffer by emanating from him, as he is a man of extremes, and I thought it quite possible that things were not as bad as they seemed.

The road from Killa Abdoola to the foot of the pass is through the bed of a mountain torrent, the low hills on either side being too far off to afford cover for anyone trying to hold the pass. The ascent to the mouth of the pass is quite gentle, and then it rises in very steep gradients 2,500 feet. We have made an excellent zig-zag road up one side and down the other, and the view from the top is very extensive and curious. About quarter to three I rode into Chaman, having come across under three hours, which was not bad, as the cavalry soldiers I had with me had already done eleven miles more, and I had to save their horses in case of necessity either for a charge or a bolt on the road. I found General Phayre much exercised in mind, and greatly impressed with the fact that there was a general, not a local, hostile movement against us. His information came from Quetta from Sir R. Sandeman, who is not, I think, as a rule very dependable in his news.

However, of one thing, there was no doubt that there had been, the night before, an attack in force on a small commissariat depot about twenty-six miles from Chaman, and that there an officer and seventeen or eighteen men (principally commissariat servants) had been killed, and that another depot, sixteen miles from Chaman, had been partially looted, but no one killed. To this depot, named Gatai, General Phayre had sent on a wing of a native regiment, and had a troop of native cavalry ready to go with me if I would go on at once there, and then act as I thought best, but he recommended my waiting at Gatai until he sent me as reinforcements two guns of a mountain battery, and a couple of hundred of the 7th Fusiliers. Of course I was all anxiety to get on, so, borrowing horses from the native cavalry for Major Greig and myself, we started again an hour after we had reached Chaman, escorted by the troop of native cavalry.

The distance between the two places is seventeen miles, and the road lies over a stony, sandy plain, without a village or a living being to be seen. I pushed on as fast as I could, as I wanted, if possible, to get to Gatai and see all the necessary arrangements for the defence of the post made before dark. On arriving, I found that all had been done by the officer in command which was possible, but the means at his disposal were very limited, and so had been his time. He had, however, closed up the greater portion of the entrance with bags of grain, and had raised the walls in a temporary fashion by laying along them rows of grain bags and making temporary loop holes. The necessary sentries and picquets were posted, but the night passed quietly, all of us, however, sleeping in our clothes.

I had no luggage, clothes, or bedding, except the breeches, and boots, and Norfolk jacket I stood in, but the officers made a subscription of blankets for me; and one young fellow insisted on my sleeping on his camp bed, which unwillingly I had to do, he was so kindly urgent about it.

Sunday, April, 18th.—Before continuing my story it will be as well to explain that between the Khojak Pass and Kandahar, the road is divided into six stages, as follows:—

1st. Chaman,	at foot of the Pass.
2nd. Gatai,	17 miles from Chaman.
3rd. Dubbrai,	10 miles from Gatai.
4th. Mel Kharez,	12 miles from Dubbrai.
5th. Abdool Rahmon,	12½ miles from Mel Kharez.
6th. Mandi Hissar,	14 miles from Abdool Rahmon.
7th. Kandahar,	11 miles from Mandi Hissar.

At each of these places there is a small enclosure, it cannot be called a fort, in which the commissariat stores are placed. General Stewart refused to garrison the smaller of these with our troops, but left them in charge of native levies who the civil authorities assured him were perfectly trustworthy. The value of this opinion has been very conclusively shown by the events of the past week. Each enclosure or fort is like the other, except in size, some being larger than others. They are of the following shape:—

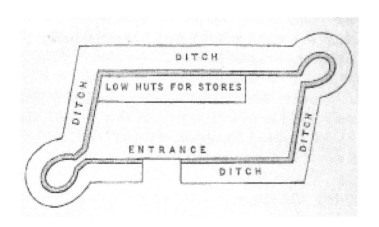

General Phayre (leaving me, however, full powers to act as I thought best) suggested to me that it would be better to wait at Gatai till the guns and the European troops reached me, but on reflection I came to the conclusion that to leave Dubbrai unoccupied, and the dead unburied a moment longer than could be avoided, would have the worst effect, and that it was quite worth risking something to obviate this, so, as soon as it was light, I issued orders (I may mention for my soldier and sailor brothers' information that I have throughout given each person distinct and plain written orders, so that everyone knew exactly what to do, and once I issued an order I never changed it) for reconnoitring parties of cavalry to proceed to Dubbrai and the hills to our right front, while I pushed on a detachment of native infantry, with a few cavalry, to reoccupy Dubbrai. I, of course, left a sufficient force at Gatai to hold it, instructing the officer in command to strengthen the defences and keep a good look out. I did not, I confess, expect opposition, and was not therefore surprised to find, when I followed the main body with a small cavalry escort, that they had found Dubbrai empty, except of dead bodies, and seen none of the enemy on the road.

We found in and around the fort thirty dead bodies and 1 wounded man, who told us he was a *Ghazi* (fanatic), from Khelat-i-Ghilzi and that there were plenty more of them coming. The men were most anxious to shoot the wretched creature, and I think the officers generally thought it would have been right to do so, but of course I forbid anything of the kind, and ordered him medical aid, and such food and drink as we had at our disposal. I am bound to say he was not a bit grateful, but regularly spit at us and defied us. He died the next day, which was quite the best thing he could have done.

Among the dead we found and recognized poor Major Waudby's body, which I buried near the place he fell, reading the funeral service myself as the best and greatest mark of respect I, as commanding the force, could give to as gallant a soldier as ever lived. Poor fellow, he had warning full eight hours before the attack, and could easily have evacuated the place, but knowing the country and natives well, he knew what an evil effect it would have if it was known a *sahib* had shown fear, and so he clearly elected to accept, one may say, certain death, rather than discredit his name. He had only two sepoys of his own regiment with him, all the rest being helpless unarmed servants of his own and the commissariat establishment. He must have fought splendidly, as the enemy themselves acknowledge that they had sixteen killed and eighteen wounded, which was very good shooting.

Nearly everyone we saw of the enemy was shot right through the head, so poor Waudby must have been as cool and collected as if he had been shooting pheasants. His two sepoys died with him, and were found beside him. We also found his dog sitting by his body refusing to be moved. The poor dog had two terrible sword cuts on his back, but is recovering, and will be sent home to Mrs. Waudby. While at Dubbrai I received a despatch from Kandahar, saying that they had sent out troops from there to open the road up to wherever they met us, and the officer in command sent me word that no resistance had been offered and I could march on in the ordinary way. I at once sent back to Chaman and countermanded the move of the guns, and gave the necessary orders for the improving of the defences of Dubbrai, and at the same time wrote to Kandahar to General Primrose, recommending that I should remain a few days in the neighbourhood with a force of cavalry, artillery and infantry, and that I should march through all the disaffected districts, as I believed this course necessary and desirable. I then rode back to Gatai, on my way going to see about the removal into safety at that place of a large quantity of Government property which one of my patrolling parties had discovered in the middle of some hills about half way between the two places. These things proved to be a large convoy of Government stores which an Afghan contractor had been bringing upon camels to Kandahar, when he was attacked by the enemy, and obliged to drop his load, and give them his camels to carry the wounded and the loot from Dubbrai. We succeeded in rescuing them and bringing them into the fort at Gatai, where I was obliged to leave them.

April 19th.—The next morning I was reinforced by some of the 7th Fusiliers, my own escort with my baggage coming in at the same time. I had been 48 hours without anything but the clothes I stood in, and I must say I really felt very little inconvenience from the want of my luxuries. The ground does not make half a bad bed, especially if one has been riding in a hot sun for twelve or fourteen hours, and as to eating and drinking there is no sauce like hunger and thirst, and under such circumstances it is wonderful how extremely nice, things, that really are very nasty, seem. I have discovered that a saddle is a first-class pillow, and that with it and a couple of blankets and a fairly soft piece of ground, a most excellent bed is quite possible. The truth was, I was really done when evening came, and any place where one could stretch oneself was delightful. On the afternoon of the 19th I rode back to Dubbrai to try to telegraph to Kandahar, taking a telegraph signaller with his instrument with me.

The enemy had again (after all my trouble of the previous day) cut the wire, and we had a lot more work to do so very unwillingly, as it was getting dark, and I had only two native cavalry soldiers with me and no officer, I was obliged to start back to Gatai without succeeding in sending my telegram. It was rather a risky ride back in the dark (I did not get back into camp till near 9 o'clock), but I kept a good look out, and always took care to be going rather hard in any confined place where the enemy could have concealed themselves. We saw not a soul, except on one occasion in an open piece of ground, I thought I made out four or five fellows about a quarter of a mile off, who, the very instant they saw I was coming towards them with my two soldiers, bolted, and I thought, under the circumstances, that I had no business to go skiing after them, so pursued my road quietly without an accident or incident of any kind.

April 20th.—This morning the wire was restored, and General Primrose telegraphed to me that it was not thought necessary to keep troops, as I suggested, at Gatai and thereabouts, and that he wanted me at Kandahar. I then thought this wrong, and still think so, and the events of the last few days have amply supported my views. However, I had nothing to do but to obey, which I did, stating, however, my views of the position very plainly in my report. The 7th Fusiliers (Head Quarters) joined me this morning full of indignation because one of their native servants, who had strayed away from the road, had been attacked by Afghans and most seriously wounded. They had sent a couple of cavalry soldiers out, who had evidently seized the first two Afghans they had met and declared them to be the culprits. There was a great demand for immediate *justice?* and I fancy the lives of the two poor wretches would not have been worth much had I not been in camp and positively prohibited anything but an enquiry, leaving the punishment of the men to the civil authorities. I was the more determined on this point, as the evidence against them seemed to me to be very weak. I marched for Mel Kharez at 4 o'clock with my usual escort and party, and stopping to dine at Dubbrai, arrived at the end of our journey (the distance is twenty-one miles) about half-past eleven. The last two hours we had a bright moon and clear cold air, and the ride was very enjoyable.

Wednesday, 21st April.—Mel Kharez has a fort like the other places, and it was also looted, but no English officer being there, the native commissariat establishment had very wisely bolted to safety, and so no one was killed. I should say that this station was, of course, more favourably situated than Dubbrai, as it was within twelve miles of a military post of ours, while Dubbrai was at least twenty-five miles away from any help. I forgot to mention an amusing little incident at Gatai. There also the commissariat agent, a Parsee, had run away when the place was attacked.

When he returned and came to me to report his arrival, I said to him in chaff, "oh, you are the gentleman who ran away!"

To which he replied quite as if he was much pleased with himself, "yes, sir, I ran away, and thereby I have saved my life," which was certainly true.

At Gatai I had much trouble in getting water, the neighbouring chiefs having cut off the stream which supplied the Fort. After exhausting all gentle means to bring them to reason, I tried the moral force of some cavalry who I sent with orders to bring the chief man before me. The officer did his work capitally, bringing back a leading native chief, whose seizure had the best effect, as the water flowed into our camp sharp enough as soon as they knew I had their head man in my power. I kept my friend as a kind of a state prisoner till the next morning, when, with the usual formalities of Eastern life, I gave him an interview.

He was a singularly handsome fine old man, with (like all true Afghans) a very Jewish type of countenance and a good manner. He was humble enough, and tried to make all sorts of excuses, none of which I informed him I thought at all good, but as the water had been turned on, and he had apologised for the delay, I dismissed him with a warning for the future. Several of the other chiefs came in to make their *salaam* to me, and to promise all sorts of things for the future. An Afghan is, however, so natural a liar that no one thinks of believing them, and among themselves they are never weak enough to put any trust one in the other, and in this they are quite wise, as a more treacherous lying set of beings do not, I suppose, exist on the face of the world.

We marched from Mel Kharez at 2 p.m., a beautiful afternoon, to Abdool Rahmon, which is 121 miles off. The road lay through an undulating valley, on the edges of which there were some signs of cultivation. Four miles from Mel Kharez is a range of hills called the Ghlo Kotal, at which we had hoped and expected the enemy would have made a stand, but they had bolted on the first sign of our troops approaching. After crossing the Kotal we descended into the Takt-i-Pul plain, and reached Abdool Rahmon about 6 o'clock. There is the usual fort at this place, and it is well and sufficiently garrisoned, and its defences are quite good enough for the requirements. Abdool Rahmon is twenty-six miles from Kandahar, so I determined I would ride in there ahead of my party next morning, leaving them with the baggage to do the distance in the usual two marches.

I got the native chief of the place, a certain Gholam Jan, to lend me a trotting camel on which to send my bag and bedding into Kandahar, and arranged to ride Rufus the first stage and a cavalry horse the last one into Kandahar. An order from Kandahar prohibits officers attempting to go alone, so I took an escort of a non-commissioned officer and four cavalry soldiers with me, the escort being relieved at the next stage.

Thursday, 22nd April.—Left Abdool Rahmon at 6.30 a.m., with an escort of five *sowars* (native cavalry), and cantered to Mandi Hissar, the next and last stage on the road to Kandahar. The country is a dead plain, with some little cultivation, and intersected by watercourses. There are numerous fortified villages dotted about, from which the passersby are very often fired upon. At Mandi Hissar I was to change my horse for a trooper from the cavalry detachment there, and also to relieve my escort. While the horse and escort were being prepared I had a talk with the old *soubadar* (native captain) commanding the detachment of the 19th Native Infantry quartered there, who, with all his men, were most anxious to hear all I could tell them about Major Waudby, who was beloved by all in the regiment. The old *soubadar* told me that they all knew what a big heart (*i.e.,* how brave) he had, and he added "if we can only meet the Afghan scoundrels, we will avenge Waudby *Sahib's* death right well;" and so I feel sure they will.

To show the feeling of this regiment I may mention that when the news of Major Waudby's death was received, a detachment of 150 men were ordered to march at once to join me. The men were told off in the usual manner, but when the detachment paraded it was found that 170 were present, twenty men having fallen in in the hopes that they would not be discovered, and would succeed in getting to the front. After leaving Mandi Hissar, the country is the usual stony, dusty desert for three or four miles, when a low range of hills are crossed, and the road descends into the valley in which Kandahar lies, which was green with corn fields and orchards, and was the pleasantest sight I had seen since I left Bombay. In the distance the grey

54

mud walls of the city of Kandahar were visible, but making no imposing appearance, and differing really in no way from the villages we had passed, except the extent was greater, and that in many places the line of the walls was hidden by the orchards which lie all round the city.

Unlike most Mahomedan cities, no domes or minarets of mosques were visible, and I believe there is in the whole place but one mosque of any importance, and it would be hardly noticed in any Mahomedan town in India. Passing round the wall of the city I was conducted by an orderly who had been sent out to meet me to the charming house in which General Primrose and his staff live, where I found a very friendly welcome, and a very good breakfast ready for me. Including a quarter of an hour's halt at Mandi Hissar, I had accomplished my ride of twenty-five miles in three and a half hours, which was sufficiently fast, as I did not want to over-ride my horses. The house occupied by the general is a regular native building, composed of small and oddly shaped rooms, very thick walls, and a flat roof.

Many of the rooms are highly ornamented with painting and gilding, and it is a quaint and cool place to live in, especially as it stands in a delightful garden full of roses, mulberries, peach, pear, plum trees, and vines, through which flow narrow canals of water with a rapid stream, and forms altogether a most delightfully quiet and refreshing sight after the wretched deserts we had been passing through. In this garden, but in another house, also lives the chief political officer, Colonel St. John, and his assistant. The garden has a wall twelve feet high round it, and the entrances are guarded by English native troops, as it is, of course, important to avoid any risks to the chief military officer. Outside the garden lie the very regiments of the force, for the greater number of whom a certain degree of shelter from the sun is provided in the shape of mud huts or buildings of Afghan pattern.

Some of the regiments are quartered in regular Afghan villages, out of which the inhabitants have been turned, but some of the buildings now occupied by troops are actually those which we built ourselves for our men when we occupied Kandahar in

1839, and which were found in fairly good condition when we returned here forty years later, in 1879. Quarters of a not very luxurious description are provided for the officers, that is to say, they are given a room without doors or windows, and with a mud floor, and any improvements they wish to make they are required to do themselves. There is, of course, no furniture, and any luxuries one wants in that way we have to get for ourselves. The room I have got is at one end of a long low line of mud huts, the whole of which, except the four rooms at one end, which are allotted to me and my staff, and the four rooms at the other end which will be given to General Burrows and his staff, are occupied by artillery officers. My set of quarters are in this shape:

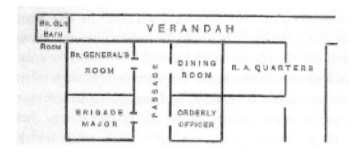

So I have one room to sleep, sit, and write in, and a room where we dine and breakfast, and which is, of course, public property. I have, as a special indulgence, a bath-room all to myself, but no one else has one. The room when I came into it was horrid; the floor was six inches deep in dust; there were no doors or windows, and altogether it was most unpromising. I have, however, had a floor made for it, the passage and dining-room, of a wonderful kind of stuff like plaster of Paris which abounds here, and which hardens in the most wonderful way. I have had windows put in, and hope to have a door soon; and having bought a few pieces of a rough native carpeting in the city, and a couple of tables and chairs, my room begins to look very fair indeed. The mud walls are appropriately covered with yards of maps, which look very business-like, and in the small recesses I have had a few wooden shelves put up which quite do to hold my very scanty wardrobe.

I find my room very hot and close at night, so I have pitched my little tent outside my door and sleep in it, watched over by a sentry whose sole duty is to guard his sleeping general, who can, therefore, slumber in the most perfect security. It would be rather monotonous to live with my brigade major and orderly officer only, as I am afraid we should get very tired of each other during the hot weather, so I am trying to get up a sort of mess between General Burrows and me, taking in our staff, and a couple of outsiders who have no special place to go to—*viz.*, our chaplain, Mr. Cane, and the judge advocate, Colonel Beville. The latter has agreed to manage the affair, so I have nothing to do with housekeeping, which is a blessing, and as Colonel Beville quite understands management and likes good things, I hope the affair will be a success, and that General Burrows will agree to join.

The parson begged me to take him in, and I did not like to refuse, though I cannot say I care much about him (though perhaps he will improve on acquaintance), as he has the reputation of being rather inclined to quarrel and be difficult to manage. We will hope he is maligned and will prove not to have so un-clerical a failing. A mess on service is a very rough affair, as we have no plate, crockery or linen, and live what is called camp fashion, that is, all the mess provides is tables and food, and each person's servant brings his plates, knives, forks, and spoons, and chairs, and when dinner or breakfast is over removes them. We shall, I daresay, in time get a few luxuries such as chairs, dishes, and perhaps a few table-cloths (I have two of my own for great occasions), and we have already made our dining-room look fairly comfortable (I am writing on 4th May), by putting down some carpets, and I have no doubt between Colonel Beville and me that we will get rid of as much unnecessary roughness as we can.

The great drawback of the whole place is the flies, which are most exasperating and pertinacious. I am preparing a complete set of fortifications against them for my own room, by having net (which I have been fortunate to get in the city), such as mosquito curtains are made of, nailed over the windows, and a door covered with net for the one entrance, so that I hope in time to be fairly free from them. They retire for the night, I am glad to say, about 7 o'clock, but as soon as they leave the sand-flies begin, and I think they are almost as bad, as they buzz and bite just like mosquitoes. They are a kind of very small gnat, and their bite is most irritating to some people, but they don't hurt me. The regiments are necessarily scattered over a large extent of ground, and the work is consequently very heavy on the men, as we have to post sentries very closely together to prevent the Afghans coming within our lines.

The great proportion of the force is outside the city where I am living, but we hold the citadel, which is inside the city, where also we keep our arsenal and commissariat stores. A native in-fantry regiment and a detachment of a British infantry regiment hold the citadel, and the quarters occupied by both the officers and men there are much preferable to ours in the cantonments, as they are all regular native houses, many of which have gar-dens, and all some trees near and about them, and in this desert land a bit of green or a little shade have a value which no one who has not seen the country can understand. There is nothing striking about the actual city of Kandahar to anyone who has visited or seen an ordinary Indian town of the 5th or 6th rank. There are the usual bazaars with the occupants of the shops at work at their various trades in the front of their shops, and in many shops coarse English earthenware and cheap Birmingham and Manchester goods are exposed for sale, as is the case in even small villages in India. Raisins of all sorts and description, from the little sultanas up to dark purple ones, are sold in quantities, and seem to be a regular portion of the food of the poorest people.

So far I have seen nothing curious or unusual which I would be tempted to buy, but then we cannot here wander about and go into the shops and ransack them for curiosities, as the people have a nasty trick of watching till a person is busy looking at things in a shop, and then coming up quietly and stabbing one in the back. It is consequently necessary, when we go shopping, to go in parties of two or three, or take an escort, so as to always have someone on the watch against treachery, and as long as one takes this precaution they are too cowardly to attack in the open. The people in the streets are very picturesque, and most of them fine handsome men. No women are ever seen except very old ones, and even they generally wear the Turkish *yashmak* or veil which covers them from head to foot. In the centre of the city the four main streets meet under a curious large-domed building, around which are shops, and which is always crowded with a very mixed gathering of villains of all sorts. This place is called the Charsoo (or four waters), and it was in it that Lieutenant Willis, of the artillery, was murdered in broad day light by a *Ghazi* (N.B.—Next week I will explain who and what *Ghazis* are), who, however, was himself immediately killed. Any native attempting the life of any officer or soldier is now always hung in the Charsoo, which has had a very good effect.

Thursday, 22nd April, continued.—The newspapers have had a good deal of late about *Ghazis*, both here and at Cabul, and I dare say it will be well to explain who and what they are, as even here people have an idea that every Afghan who fights against us is a *Ghazi*, and there is some reason for this idea, as the primary meaning of the Persian word is "a warrior." The *Ghazis*, however, with whom we have had to deal, are fanatical Mahomedans who bind themselves by vows to kill one or more of the infidels (that is of us), and thereby earn a positive certainty of going straight to heaven. So convinced are they that if they can only kill an infidel their future happiness is secured, that they are perfectly indifferent as to whether they lose their own life in the attempt or not, in fact I believe they rather desire to be killed, and so enter at once on all the delights of a Mahomedan Paradise, the principal charm of which is, that they are there to have as many wives as ever they like, all, we will hope, warranted free from vice or temper, and requiring no management, but living as a happy family, without any jealousy or inclination to scratch out each others' eyes, as I fear would be the case in a similar establishment on earth.

It will be easily understood that a gentleman with these ideas in his head is a very awkward customer, as, caring absolutely nothing as to what happens to himself, he has a very great pull over the man he attacks, who is extremely unwilling to be either wounded or killed. Moreover, although the *Ghazis* are undoubtedly brave to foolhardiness, they don't at all disdain stratagem or treachery, and much prefer to stab their first victim quietly in the back, as the more men they kill before they are themselves killed, by so much the more is their position in Paradise improved. They, however (that is the real *Ghazis*), never use fire-arms, only swords or long Afghan knives, and always try for a personal hand-to-hand encounter. There have been many cases of attacks by *Ghazis* here, and though in every case the *Ghazi* was immediately himself killed, nothing seemed to stop the practice.

There has, however, been no attempt of the kind for a month, but of course none of the necessary precautions are relaxed. The last case was that of a lad, who was a sworn *Ghazi*, attacking an officer with no other weapon than a shoemaker's awl, with which, however, he inflicted a couple of disagreeable wounds in the back before he was seen and seized. On Christmas day five men walked out of the city, and came into the barracks of the 59th, and (in open day) produced long knives from under their clothes, called out that they were *Ghazis*, and had come to kill anyone they could get at. Of course they were shot down, but so wild was the shooting that four of the men of the regiment were killed by the bullets from their comrades' rifles! The incident, however, shows what plucky fellows they are, as of course when they entered the barracks of the 59th, and openly declared their purpose, they must have known their lives were forfeited. In consequence of the number of *Ghazis* here, and the generally hostile feelings of the people to us, we are all required to go armed at all times, even when riding out or walking for exercise.

It is a great worry, and I hate it, being a little sceptical as to the necessity for the extreme measure of precaution required, and am disposed to think a neat little bludgeon of a walking stick I possess would prove a much more serviceable defence to me than my regulation sword. Everyone carries loaded revolvers, especially when in the city, and I dare say the fact that we all do so being known, prevents many attempted attacks being made. The soldiers have to carry their rifles, and when they go into the town have to fix their bayonets, and altogether we live in a regular state of siege, which I would myself like to see ended by the application of some good strong remedies, and immediate and severe punishment for murderous attacks. Still, even then I fear we could not hope to change the nature of an Afghan, who is born a treacherous, lying, murdering scoundrel. Strong words, I know, but nothing more than they deserve, as even their admirers can say nothing in favour of their moral qualities.

Friday, 23rd April.—Being, for the present, the next senior officer to General Primrose, I exercise the command of all the troops at Kandahar, and all local arrangements and details are in my hands, as General Primrose commands the whole force, the senior officer at each place having the local command. When General Burrows arrives the command here devolves, by virtue of his seniority, on him, and I fall back on my brigade command, which I hold now in conjunction with the large command. The troops here form a nice little force, and consist of—

3 Batteries of artillery.
2 Native cavalry regiments.
2 British infantry regiments.
3 Native infantry regiments.
And sappers and miners.

And though the command entails plenty of work and responsibility, I like it, and wish I could keep it while I am here. The first thing, of course, was to ascertain the positions held by various regiments, their weak points, &c, and so I spent the afternoon in riding round and making myself acquainted with everything as far as I could, so that in case of a row at night, I should be ready to decide on what might be necessary to do. I moved into my quarters in the cantonments, and obtained permission for Captain Law, of the artillery, to act as my brigade-major, as the officer who is to hold the appointment permanently has not yet arrived. Captain Law is a smart good officer, and I am very glad to have him as my staff officer.

Saturday, 24th April.—This afternoon I was greatly delighted to receive orders to hold in readiness a small force to proceed into the Arghesan valley, to disperse a considerable gathering of the enemy who were reported to be there. I was to go in command, so I had a double interest in the matter, and lost no time in seeing that everything was prepared, and that we should be fully supplied with all the necessary appliances for entrenching, road and bridge making, blowing up the enemy's forts, &c. We were not to start till Monday, and then only if the enemy did not agree to disperse and submit to the Governor of Kandahar, which they had been called on to do. I am sorry to say that hearing of our preparations they gave in at once, and eventually my little expedition was countermanded, which was a great disappointment to everyone.

During the evening we had a little excitement, as an Afghan tried to steal and run away with the rifle of one of the native soldiers, which he had put down on the ground for a minute. The soldier gave the alarm, and four men of the nearest guard turned out and, after an exciting chase of about three miles, they came up within 400 yards of the thief, who immediately fired at them, but they returned his fire with good effect, and killed him at the 2nd shot, recovering the rifle and the remainder of the ammunition.

Sunday, 25th April.—We had (as we have each Sunday) service for the troops in the open. The men are formed up on three sides of a square, and a pile of drums on the fourth side acts as reading desk and pulpit. Of course the men come with their

rifles, and everyone is fully armed, ready for business at a moment's notice. There is a room in one of the barracks where evening service is held, but it is too small for the whole of the men in the morning, and there is also a temporary church in the citadel, where there is service morning and evening performed by a missionary.

April 26th to 30th.—I was engaged morning and afternoon visiting all the regiments, camps and hospitals, and making myself thoroughly acquainted with the various positions, and carrying out such changes and alterations as seemed to me necessary, first, for the safety of the place, and next for the comfort of the men. I also managed to take a few gallops out along the main roads which lead to Herat and Ghuzni, so as to have some idea of the country, in case of necessity. I hope shortly to know every inch of the country for ten or fifteen miles round, but this will take a little time. I am required by General Primrose never to move about with less than two native cavalry soldiers, and of course if I go more than four or five miles from camp I would take four.

Sometimes I take my brigade-major or orderly officer, or both, but I like best wandering about alone, as then I feel more independent (that is without any other officer). Frequently, however, parties of six or seven officers are got up, and we have a scamper across country, earnestly hoping we may meet someone who would like to try conclusions with us.

Saturday, May 1.—Received letters from home, dated 1st April, a most welcome arrival and a great pleasure. People who get letters every day in the week cannot understand what the pleasure of getting letters is when you can only hear once a week, and then only provided the Afghans have been behaving themselves along the road.

Sunday, May 2.—I had just settled myself down to a quiet day after service and breakfast when a report was brought to me that there had been a row in the city between the Afghans and some soldiers of the artillery, and that two soldiers had been shot and one wounded. There was a good deal of excitement, as

everyone at once made up their minds that it was the beginning of an organized attack. The accounts which I succeeded in getting out of the soldiers who had rushed up out of the city were most conflicting, excepting in one remarkable point on which all agreed, and that was that only one shot had been heard, although it was acknowledged that one of our men fired off his carbine down the street.

This was curious, and made me doubtful about the whole affair, so I sent the brigade-major off to the city at once to discover the facts for me, and went over to General Primrose, who sent the political officer also into the city to make enquiries, and eventually we ascertained, almost without a doubt, that the men had been killed by the accidental discharge of a carbine by one of their comrades who had been fiddling with his loaded carbine, which had gone off, and the bullet passing through two men killed them instantaneously. Since then the man has confessed and explained the whole matter, and there is now no doubt that there was no shot fired by the Afghans at all. The affair caused some excitement, and might have led to very serious results.

May 3rd, 4th, & 5th.—More inspections and visits to the troops morning and evening which fully occupied my time.

May 6.—A party of officers, among whom was William French, accompanied me to visit the valley of the Argandab River, which lies N.E. and N.W., and about four miles from Kandahar. To get to this valley a range of hills rising to 4,500 feet (that is 1,000 feet higher than our camp) has to be crossed, there being only two practicable passes, and these very rough, steep, and bad. The change from the dusty stone plain round Kandahar to the valley, which lies on the other side of these hills, is extraordinary, as nothing can be more wretched than the one and nothing more charming than the other. The whole valley is a series of fields of the most magnificent crops of wheat and barley, meadows full of clover, and orchards of every imaginable description of fruit. (To be continued).

May 6th.—It would not be possible to give an idea of the luxuriance of the crops and the extraordinary abundance and variety of the fruits in the Argandab valley. Every field has rows of mulberry trees round, which were covered with fruit, of which the passersby (we among them) eat apparently as much as they like without payment. The other fruits were not ripe, but the apricots were just beginning to get soft, as were the plums, especially one very like the greengage in appearance and taste. Besides these there were vines everywhere, climbing over the walls and up the mulberry and other trees, all covered with a magnificent promise of grapes.

There were also in abundance—peaches, nectarines, figs, pears, apples, quinces, and pomegranates, the latter being only in flower, but in that way adding greatly to the general appearance of the orchards, as they bear a very dark red flower which is most effective among the dark green of their leaves. Each field or orchard has a rapidly flowing stream of clear cool water running through it, which is the cause of the extreme luxuriance of everything, and very grateful to us who have been so long in a very "dry and thirsty land." (The remarkable fitness of these Bible descriptions are very clearly seen in these eastern lands). After halting in a mulberry grove resting our horses and having a good feed of mulberries, we struck out across country to get home, and had a delicious ride along the banks of a big canal shaded with trees, and felt very sorry when we emerged once again into the dust and glare of Kandahar. The apricots are now (May 12th) just being brought into the market, and we buy them (paying, no doubt, an extravagant price) for 1½d. For 2 lbs.!! The difficulty is to avoid eating too many. Peaches, plums, and figs, will follow, and we shall, I believe, have grapes in June.

The people are now cutting their corn which is rapidly ripening, which we are sorry for, as we shall miss the beautiful green they now are, and have only fields of yellow stubble. The primitive reaping hook, almost exactly similar to that used at home, is in use here, and the Afghan spade is almost similar to our shovel in shape, with the exception that on the handle of the shovel a cross piece of wood is fixed as a foot piece for the digger. I am told, but this I can hardly believe, that from the same root of wheat, barley, and oats (that is from one sowing), they get in this country two distinct crops, and certainly they appear systematically to cut down the first crop when it is green, but after it has eared, and in a few weeks afterwards a second crop is in ear without any fresh sowing.

May 7th.—Rode out to visit the old city of Kandahar, which has been in ruins since 1737 when it was besieged by the Persian King, Nadir Shah, and after a long siege taken and destroyed. It is a curious sight to see it now, as the walls of the city and many of the fortifications, which must have been for those days very strong, still remain in wonderful preservation, as do the Avails of the houses covering a considerable extent of ground, but not a living soul is to be seen, and the whole place is a picture of desolation and loneliness. After Nadir Shah had destroyed this city, he caused another one, also fortified, to be built about four miles off, but this also has been deserted, and is even more ruined than the older city. The present city of Kandahar is the third which has been built within the last 150 years.

May 8th.—I made an excursion to one of the Passes over the hills near this, but the distance was longer than I had calculated on, and as it was getting dark I had to turn home without accomplishing my object.

May 9th.—I started for a ride at half-past 5 p.m., accompanied by my usual escort of two native cavalry soldiers, and proposed to myself to ride to a place called Kokeran, about seven miles off. When I got out about two miles on the road I saw that there were threatenings of a dust-storm from that direction, and, not caring to ride for pleasure into a cloud of dust, I turned off to the left and took a canter for three or four miles through the fields, coming out eventually on the Kokeran road, about four miles from our camp. The weather had cleared then, and I thought I might still have time to explore a little way along this road, but on looking at my watch I found it was 7 o'clock, and that (as there is no twilight here) it would be quite dark before I could get home, so I turned round and cantered back to camp.

Just as I got close to the camp of the 19th Native Infantry, I saw a party of officers and two cavalry soldiers going along very slowly in front of me, and on riding up to them and enquiring what was the matter, I found that they, while returning along the Kokeran road from a ride, had been fired on by a party of Afghans concealed behind a wall, and that one officer (Captain Garrett) and one *sowar* were badly wounded. Captain Garrett was nearly fainting and falling off his horse, as he had to ride about five miles after being wounded, so I got him off on to the ground, and supported him till a doctor and a litter to carry him in was brought, and at the same time sent off one of the officers to report the occurrence to General Primrose. The attack had taken place about a mile nearer to Kokeran than the spot at which I had come out on the road, so, had I been half an hour or even less earlier arriving there, I should certainly have gone down the road, and had a chance of a scrimmage on my own account, and had I carried out my original intention I should have got to the spot where the ambuscade was before the other party, or possibly just about the same time, which would have been more convenient altogether.

My first inclination when I heard the account was to gallop back to the place with my own two *sowars* and the one unwounded man of the party which had been attacked, but on reflection for an instant I felt this would not be correct, first, because I was bound to take General Primrose's orders, next because the chances were, that long before I could get back the five miles the attacking party would have run away, and lastly that it would certainly be considered not the place of a general to be scampering with three men over the country like a cavalry subaltern, and so I galloped off to General Primrose in the hopes he would give me the cavalry brigade and let me go off to scour the whole country.

At first he was very well inclined to do this, but eventually less forward councils prevailed and a hundred good? reasons were discovered for doing nothing till morning. On further enquiring from the officers who were fired at, we found that they had been out to Kokeran, and were riding quietly back, the three officers abreast and the two *sowars* behind, when suddenly a volley was fired at them, and thinking there was a large body of men concealed, they galloped off. As it turned out there were only ten or twelve men, and after seeing the ground as I did next morning, I had no difficulty in coming to the conclusion that they might, with good effect, have halted some 200 or 300 yards off, and returned the fire with good success.

May 10.—I went out very early with some cavalry and the political officer, and scoured the country round, but of course found no traces of the party who had fired on the officers, and all the surrounding villages absolutely denied any complicity in the affair, so we had to return to camp, having been unable to. accomplish anything. In the afternoon I went out again with an escort of cavalry, and accompanied by five or six officers, and we went to Kokeran and hunted the hills all round, but saw no one. No doubt we threw away our only chance in deferring till today what ought to have been done yesterday.

May 11th.—I attended a great *durbar* (or court) at the palace of the Governor, in the city, at which the letter appointing Shere Ali Khan, Governor of the Province of Kandahar, on behalf of the Queen, was to be read. Although it was very like what all such affairs in India are, it was quite worth seeing, and I should have enjoyed it very much if I had not been obliged to eat and drink so many nasty things as Persian etiquette on such occasions absolutely requires one to swallow.

The proceedings commenced with small cups of tea, without milk or cream, being handed round, then there were speeches and the presentation of the Viceroy's letter, and of the presents sent by the Queen, and the affair wound up by trays of Afghan sweet-meats and iced sherbet being brought in, of which all, even the soldiers on the guard of honour, were required to partake. Iced sherbet sounds nice, but when it is flavoured with musk, it is apt (at least as far as I am concerned) to act very like an emetic. The sweetmeats I dare say I should have appreciated better about thirty or forty years ago, and my orderly officer certainly seemed to find them very much to his taste. I send a capital account of the whole affair which appeared in the *Kandahar News,* and which can be read by those curious in such matters at this point.

On the 13th of May the new Governor, or as he is called here, the *Wali,* which is the Persian word for Governor of a province, announced his intention of coming to pay a return visit of ceremony to General Primrose, and as Government wished us to show him all possible honour we had the whole garrison out (about 5,000 men) and lined the streets of the town and the roads between his palace and General Primrose's house. The troops turned out wonderfully well and smartly, and we hear the Governor and his people were much impressed by their appearance. After seeing all right along the line of the procession I returned to General Primrose's house, where all the staff were collected to assist General Primrose in receiving his guest.

The *Wali* (or Governor) arrived about 5 to 6 o'clock, accompanied by a very ragged looking lot of followers. He sat between General Primrose and me, and we had to carry on the usual uninteresting exchange of compliments through an interpreter, as none of us could speak Persian, and none of the Afghans could speak Hindustani. After a short time tea was handed round, and to our relief the visit, which was necessarily a very stupid affair, ended. According to Eastern etiquette, the Governor ought to have brought return presents with him, and each of us who were there should have had some present, but our government do not allow us to accept anything of value, so nothing was offered.

Since then, however, the Governor has sent us each, as a memento of the occasion, one of the new gold coins which he has struck for general issue. It is rather a pretty coin, of quite pure gold, and will do very well as an ornament for a watch chain.

May 14th to 19th.—Nothing of any interest occurred, except that I daily take long rides and increase my knowledge of the country, nearly every yard of which, for ten or twelve miles round, I have now ridden over. To the north and east of Kandahar there are very pleasant rides indeed, through green fields and shady lanes, along watercourses, but on the other two sides it is all sandy and stony deserts, with high rocky hills, which only a sense of duty has induced me to visit at all. Among other places I have been to is a gold mine which has been worked for centuries, and is situated about five miles from Kandahar. It is now, however, deserted, as the upper earth fell in two or three years ago, and has choked up the place where they say the vein of gold was.

The new Governor of Kandahar is most anxious to re-open the works, but despite the wonderful stories of the richness of the mine which the natives tell, he has not been able to get much encouragement out of our professional geologist, who, after a careful examination, has come to the conclusion that the mine will never again pay its working expenses. The morning I rode over to see the place I found the *Wali* (governor) down in the bottom of the mine, with half a dozen natives, carefully examining the place and collecting specimens, &c. He had evidently come out to have a quiet look at his new property, and did not seem particularly pleased at being caught, although he was very friendly and civil, of course.

In my wanderings through the country I never fail to investigate the quality of the fruit, and have made a discovery, in two places, of a very superior kind of mulberry, of which there appears to be only half a dozen trees in the whole valley. They are so different from the common kinds that the natives call them Shah-toot, which means, the King mulberry, and the trees they grow on are considered quite curiosities. It certainly is a very delicious fruit, and I have only revealed my discoveries to a chosen few. I am a much earlier riser than most of my friends, and therefore seldom or never have any companion in my morning rides, except the two native cavalry soldiers who are my escort.

I generally start when I have no parades or inspections, about half-past five in the morning, when the air is deliriously cool, and seldom get home till 9 o'clock, by which time the sun is very hot. The country is intersected with water channels for irrigation purposes, and mud walls divide the fields of corn and wheat, so there is lots of jumping, and some of the obstacles are very awkward. The orchards and vineyards are surrounded with very high walls, but there is also lots of fruit of all kinds growing along the paths which anyone may eat. In this country, from one end of it to another, there is no such thing as what we would call a road, as there being not a single wheeled vehicle in the whole length and breadth of the land, roads are not at all necessary. Everything is carried on camels, ponies, bullocks and donkeys, a regular stream of which flow into Kandahar every morning, loaded with fruit, grain and grass.

The people here must be making fortunes, and certainly ought to like us, as we pay anything they ask for everything, and the prices, though not very exorbitant, are at least double what they used to be. It is getting very hot now in the daytime, and we have constant dust-storms, which are, of all things, the most horrid and the greatest trial to one's temper. Imagine the delights of an immense cloud of dust a mile square, or more, driven along by a red hot wind, and forcing its way into every hole and corner. While it is passing it is quite dark, even in midday, and when it is gone everything one possesses, every table, chair and book is covered with an inch of dust, and one's hair and beard turned into a whitey brown colour, and stiff with dirt.

Here we sometimes have a dust-storm which is continuous for an hour, but generally they come up in regular succession, each lasting three or four minutes, and a shorter or longer interval between each. Towards 8 o'clock in the evening the wind goes down and it becomes quite cool, and we generally have our dinner table placed outside our quarters, and so brilliant has the moon been, that for the last four days we have dined quite comfortably by the light of it without any candles or lamps at all.

Our mess now consists of General Burrows and his Brigade-Major, Captain Heath; General Brooke, his brigade-major, Captain Leckie, and his orderly officer, Lieutenant Fox; Colonel Beville, deputy judge advocate, who manages the mess for us, Captain Harris, the deputy assistant quartermaster general, and Mr. Cane, the chaplain. The mess is managed on what is called the "camp fashion" principles—that is, everyone has to provide their own plates, cups, knives, forks, and spoons, and chair; then wine, beer, and tea at breakfast are supplied by each person for himself, according to his own taste, the mess merely providing the eatables. It is a very good plan, as then no large supplies of crockery, glass, stores, or wine are necessary, and each one is able at a moment's notice to go off on a march, with all his things complete, without interfering with the comfort of the remainder of the party.

May 20th.—A *Ghazi* attempted to kill a soldier of the 66th Foot today, but only succeeded in wounding him, and was himself instantly killed by the soldiers who happened to be near, who bayoneted him promptly. It seems that the man who was wounded was walking with a comrade down one of the streets of Kandahar, looking at the things in the shops, when an Afghan armed with a bayonet rushed out of a side street, shouted out he was a *Ghazi*, and made straight at the two men, and succeeded in inflicting two wounds (not serious) on the man nearest to him before his comrade fully realized what was happening, when he immediately bayoneted the *Ghazi*.

When I first arrived here the men used to go into the city with loose ammunition, and often, I make no doubt, with loaded rifles, and when attacked by *Ghazis* used to fire wildly and, as a rule, missed the *Ghazi*, and killed unoffending passersby. I took the loose ammunition from them (leaving them, of course, ammunition in the usual bundles in their pouches), and told them in such cases to use their bayonets first, and then, if pressed, they might open ammunition and use it. The change was not altogether liked, but this affair (the first in which a *Ghazi* has had prompt justice meted to him) has satisfactorily proved the propriety of the arrangement.

May 21st to 25th.—Nothing new has occurred. We had lots of dust-storms, but, alas, there is nothing new about them, as they come with a painful degree of regularity every afternoon.

May 26th.—There was another attempt by a *Ghazi* today to earn martyrdom, but this time it was one of the Hindustani camp followers who was attacked. He, however, had a sort of sickle in his hand, with which he was cutting some grass, and when attacked by the *Ghazi*, who had a sword, he returned the compliment so smartly that the capture of the *Ghazi* by a couple of native soldiers who came up at the moment was very easy. He was brought in a prisoner, and when his case was being investigated, and he was asked for his defence, he said simply "that he was a *Ghazi*, that he had sold his cow to buy a sword, and he was very sorry he had not killed the infidel." He was handed over to the provost marshal for immediate execution, and he accepted his fate with the most perfect coolness and indifference.

May 26th, 27th, and 28th.—Nothing of interest occurred.

May 29th.—We had a great parade for the Queen's birthday, all the troops at Kandahar being on the ground, making a very effective show, as we had three batteries of artillery, three regiments of cavalry, five regiments of infantry, and the line was of good extent. General Primrose commanded the parade, and General Burrows and I had each our own brigades. One of the performances on the Queen's birthday parade is firing a *feu de joie* with blank ammunition, when the fire is run down the whole of the front rank, and then back up the rear rank, and this is done three times, and is, as may be imagined, most trying to horses, especially those who have to stand with their backs to the line as those of the generals and staff have to do on this occasion. Prudence suggested to me to ride my old and tried charger Rufus, but vanity got the better of prudence, and being anxious to show off Akhbar, and also to make the best turnout on my own account that I could, I made up my mind to ride the Arab, who is really a picture when got up for parade.

He is young and inexperienced, and had never been on parade before, or never heard a shot fired, but Arabs very often don't mind anything of that kind, and I hoped for the best and thought it all right when he stood like a post while the artillery were firing their salute. The *feu de joie,* and the consternation it produced among all the other horses, was too much for his nerves, and he gave me all I knew to sit on him, though I don't blame him a bit, as this particular kind of firing is most trying to all horses. On this occasion not one of them really stood it steadily, and General Burrows' horse was so objectionable as to succeed in throwing him, although he is a first-rate rider. I was, however, quite repaid for the little bother I had by the admiration Mr. Akhbar's appearance called forth as he went past the saluting flag at the head of the brigade.

May 30th and 31st.—Nothing new.

June 1st and 2nd.— Do. do.

June 3rd.—I had been for some time meditating an exploring trip up a valley which had not been previously visited, and about which I wanted to know something, but had put it off from day to day on account of the heat, as the distance made it necessary to be out all the forenoon. Tired, however, of the monotony of the previous week, I determined to carry out my intention and have an outing and a good ride. I made up a party, but at the last moment all, except Captain Law and Captain Slade of the artillery, both of whom are enterprising fellows, and always ready for anything, cried off on one excuse or other, the real truth, however, being that they were too lazy and did not like the idea of a thirty-five mile ride.

At the last moment a young subaltern of the artillery asked me to let him go also, so we started a party of four officers and my two native cavalry soldiers. We took a feed for our horses and materials for a picnic breakfast with us, as we intended to halt for a couple of hours or so about 8 o'clock. We left our quarters at 4 a.m., and it was really quite chilly when we started, and continued so till quarter past 6 o'clock, when the sun got up and quickly made himself felt. Our road lay through a narrow valley, with high hills on either side, and very stony rough going it was, as, in accordance with the customs of this country, there was nothing that one could call a road or even a pathway, and consequently we had to go slowly except when now and then we got out on a bit of grassy ground where we could have a canter.

We saw a good number of deer who seemed much astonished to see a white face, and moved away from us very leisurely, making us wish we had brought a gun or rifle with us. We thought of trying our pistols on them, but did not care to throw away our ammunition unnecessarily. We also saw, though at some little distance from us, the finest eagle I have ever seen. Indeed I have never seen such an enormous bird anywhere. Our destination was a fortified village called Mansurabad, which is about fifteen miles in a straight line from Kandahar, but the turnings of the road added at least a couple of miles to that. We hit it off all right, and went all through it, the people seeming civil enough, but very anxious for us to move on.

The most of the inhabitants were out in their fields cutting a most magnificent crop of barley, wheat, and oats, and they were evidently a well-to-do lot, as there were great flocks of cattle and sheep grazing all round, and the orchards were stocked with fruit of all kinds. At this village we came on the Argandab River, from which the water, which turns the country along its banks and round Kandahar into a garden, is brought by a wonderful system of canals which carry it in all directions. These canals leave the river just below Mansurabad, and the way they are planned and engineered show great cleverness on the part of the people who made them many hundred years ago. Leaving Mansurabad behind, we struck down the valley of the Argandab, and set to work to find a good place for our halt for breakfast. This was not quite so easy to do, as we wanted such a lot of things. First and foremost, remembering the Prince Imperial's fate (though I don't think we had a Captain Carey in our party), we wanted a place which could not be approached suddenly by the wiley Afghan, and a place that if attacked we could have

75

defended ourselves in.

Then we wanted shade for ourselves and horses, and water at hand for the horses and for drinking and cooking. Eventually we got rather a good spot though we had to sacrifice shade somewhat to the other more material points. Having set our horses to work at their corn, we turned out the contents of our wallets (my campaigning saddle carries two side bags and a pair of holster wallets) and found we had the makings of a capital breakfast. My contribution was first and most important, a small kettle to boil water in, a tin of chocolate and milk, two tins of potted beef and ham, a loaf of bread, six hard-boiled eggs, salt, pepper, &c. Among the others there were more eggs and more bread, a Bologna sausage, and a heap of sandwiches.

We soon collected some sticks and had a fire burning (I had brought matches and some old newspapers), and quickly had hot water ready and chocolate made, and made an excellent breakfast, finished off by a heap of apricots brought to us by a friendly Afghan. His idea of our powers of disposing of apricots was magnificent, as, after we and our two soldiers had eaten all we possibly could (and we did our best), we fed our horses on them, and still left a good pile behind us. In this part of the world apricots are in millions, and our friend brought us a few for breakfast in a sack thrown over his shoulder. The reason why apricots are cultivated up here is that there is great demand for them in India in a dried state, and tons of them are dried in the sun and sent down to India, and can be purchased in the smallest and most remote village in that country, and you (the children) used to eat them stewed very often when you were in India, and, if I don't mistake, liked them very much. They are often called in India *Alubokaras,* which, however, is not their proper name.

We lounged about for a couple of hours, and then continued our ride down the Argandab Valley, and for ten miles rode along a charming rapidly flowing stream of clear water, well shaded on both sides by trees covered with apricots, plums, and mulberries, a most enjoyable ride, as, though the sun was hot, there was a very cool breeze, and the trees kept the great power of the sun from us. We saw many vineyards with a great promise of grapes, but none are ripe yet, and also lots of figs, apples, pears and pomegranates, all, however, some weeks from being eatable. The people we met, though not actually glad to see us, were not uncivil, and many of them offered us fruit as we rode along. No doubt our being well armed helped to make them civil.

We got home at quarter past 1 o'clock, having been nine and a quarter hours away, and having, had a most enjoyable excursion. The distance was, I think, between thirty-three and thirty-five miles, and my old friend Rufus carried me like a bird, although with my saddle bags, big saddle and all, I am afraid I made up a good fifteen stone for him to carry.

June 4th, 5th, 6th, 7th.—Nothing important occurred on the 4th, but on each of the next three days there were attempts by *Ghazis* to kill some of our people. In the two first cases the men attacked were native servants, in the third case it was a soldier of the 66th. Both the natives were seriously wounded, but the soldier having some suspicions was on his guard, and escaped with a slight scratch, and bayoneted his assailant. The last idea the *Ghazis* have taken up, which is rather a mean one, is to send quite young boys to make the attack, as naturally people neither notice the approach of, nor try to avoid a small boy, and besides men hesitate to deal out summary justice, even in self defence, on a child.

One boy who tried to stab one of our native servants is really quite a child, but as savage untamed a little viper as I ever saw. It is very hard to know how to deal with the young rascal, but I think a good whipping in a public place every other day for a month would be the best punishment. The first well authenticated account of a *Ghazi* that I know of will be found in the 3rd chapter of *Judges*, verses 14—22, as the motives and actions there described are exactly those of the *Ghazis* of today. However, this last device of sending children to do the work of men is so mean, that any little respect one might have for the motives which make men *Ghazis* is entirely destroyed.

77

June 8th.—Shortly after I left Bombay I found I should want some clothes I had left packed up, ready to follow, so I tele-graphed to Alfred Christopher, and asked him to send my port-manteau to me, and I took all sorts of precautions by writing to the various transport officers along the road, and asking them to expedite its movements. It left Bombay on the 8th April, and exactly two months later it made its appearance here, so it had travelled very leisurely, and worse still, had been cut open and nearly everything in it abstracted. All the things I most wanted were stolen, and nothing was left except my Ulster and a few pair of old drawers. When the weather gets cold I shall be very glad to have the Ulster, of course, but the loss of a first-class pair of corduroy breeches and all my warm clothing is very tiresome. This misfortune, and the destruction of my things in the Bolan River leaves me rather short of clothes, and I shall not find it easy to keep up a very respectable appearance much, longer.

June 9th, 10th, 11th.—Nothing new. The heat is very much greater the last few days, and even the nights now begin to be hot.

June 11th to 18th.—Nothing of any interest occurred, except that day by day the weather became hotter, and we lost our cool nights which had, up to this time, quite compensated for the heat of the days. A careful record of the heat during the month of June showed that the thermometer on one occasion rose in the shade to 124°, but that the average maximum for the month was 114°, and the average minimum 65°. Although the heat has, no doubt, been very great, it has not equalled in oppressiveness and debilitating effect the heat one gets at Cawnpore and Alla-habad, and stations in the Punjab. Daily the grapes and fruit have been getting riper, and we have had a sort of compensation for the heat in the variety and goodness of the fruit.

A great number of officers have been ailing more or less, the result, I am sure, of the sedentary lazy lives they lead. Great heat is, of course, enervating, and it takes some determination after a long hot night to start off for a good ride, and it is even worse in the evening. I am glad to say I have steadily stuck to my exercise, and have frequently, in the morning before breakfast, done twenty to twenty-five miles, and then eight or ten in the evening. Whatever has been the cause, I have certainly been wonderfully well, and, beyond the inconveniences of the heat, have not felt the slightest bad effects. I have now visited every inch of country within twelve to fifteen miles of Kandahar, and know every part of it thoroughly.

June 19th.—It was decided to send the 30th Native Infantry to Kelat-i-Ghilzi to relieve the 29th Native Infantry, and both regiments being in my brigade, General Primrose allowed me to march up to Kelat-i-Ghilzi with one regiment and come back with the other, going up the Argandab Valley and returning by the valley of the Tarnak. As very little was known of the Argandab route, I was very glad to have the opportunity of seeing it and also visiting Kelat-i-Ghilzi. Captain Leckie, my brigade major, was to accompany me, and Major Leach, of the engineers, on surveying duty, and Mr. Gordon, a missionary who is here, also asked to join my party. The first there was no difficulty about, but the advisability of the latter going was more doubtful. However, as he wanted to make the trip only with the view to holding services, &c, for the English troops at Kelat-i-Ghilzi, he was allowed to come, and we all made our preparations for a start on the 25th, but between the 20th and that date the heat increased so greatly that it was considered unwise for us to move until a change in the weather set in, and so, to my great disgust, our trip was postponed.

25th, 26th, 27th, 28th.—Heat very great.

29th.—We got further, and apparently more Certain information that Ayoub Khan with his army was actually on the march from Herat towards Kandahar, and preparations were at once put in hands to equip a force for despatch to Girishk to prevent his entrance into the Province of Kandahar. The distance from Herat to Girishk is 280 miles, and the road is, like all roads in this country, extremely bad, and very little water to be found along it once the Valley of the Helmund is left. About half way between Herat and Girishk is the town of Farrah, and to this place it was said Ayoub Khan's advance guard had arrived. The *Wali* of Kandahar was at Girishk, with part of his forces across the Helmund in Zamindawur, and on hearing of Ayoub Khan's movements he wrote and asked us to come to his help. Reference, of course, had to be made to the Viceroy and commander-in-chief at Simla, and in the meantime our preparations for a move went on.

The force to go out was a brigade of cavalry under General Nuttall, and a brigade of infantry under General Burrows, who, being senior, would command the force. A battery of horse artillery was also ordered to be in readiness. Generals Burrows and Nuttall being senior to me, it was natural and right that they should have the commands, and indeed in any case, of course, the cavalry general must have gone with his own brigade, but, all the same, I cannot help being envious of their luck, though I shall have most responsible and interesting work here, as on me devolves the command of the Kandahar garrison, and the task of guarding, with a force reduced much below what is desirable, the whole position here. I shall only have for this purpose two of the infantry regiments of my brigade, one of which is weak, having detachments at the posts on the Quetta road, two batteries of artillery, and about 300 cavalry. We expect two more infantry regiments up in about a fortnight, but till then we are certainly much below our proper strength.

June 30th.—The very worst dust-storm I have yet been in occurred today, as it blew from 12 o'clock till 3 a.m. on the 1st July, when the wind changed, and a most perceptible difference in the temperature occurred. Nothing could be more disagreeable than these fifteen hours were, but the change in the heat quite repaid us for the previous discomforts. Orders were received from Simla to send the proposed force to Girishk at once, so the cavalry brigade will march on the 4th, and the remainder of the force on the 5th, a junction being effected on arrival, near Girishk. Girishk is about ninety miles from Kandahar, and the road is, for the most part, through dry uncultivated country, and there would not have been sufficient water at all the halting places for the combined cavalry and infantry brigades.

Girishk is on the River Helmund, and General Burrows has positive orders not to cross that river, and I can hardly suppose it possible that Ayoub Khan will venture to force the passage of the river against our vastly superior (in arms and discipline) force. In numbers, of course, he has, it is said, about ten times a larger force than we have, but that is not of much consequence. Putting aside as unlikely his making an attempt to cross the Helmund at Girishk, three courses are open to him. The first, and it is thought by the political people the most probable, is, that on arriving near Girishk he will endeavour to come to terms with us, and put in his claim for the *Amirship*, and say he does not want to fight.

The next is, that instead of making for Girishk, he might cross the Helmund, at, or near, a place you will see on the map called *Kala Bust,* and giving General Burrows the slip, come down the Argandab to Kandahar. This, though the most unlikely, is what I should like. The third course is to pass along to the north of Girishk and cross the Helmund near *Garm-ab* (hot water), and bearing away northwards, pass along the Valley of the Tirin River, and eventually strike the Ghuzni road beyond Kelat-i-Ghilzi, and so get to Kabul without coming into collision with us at all. If Ayoub Khan does not want either to fight or make terms, or does not fall back on Herat, on finding us in force at Girishk, this last course seems a very likely one for him to take.

These being the various alternatives, we ought, according to my idea, to have a small force in the Argandab Valley, near the junction of that river with the Helmund, and we should have a strong Brigade in the Tirin Valley, but both these moves are impossible, as we have no men, and it will take all we have to hold our own here. Of course, all is, at present, conjecture, and it might even be, so defective is our information, that Ayoub Khan is still at Herat, or, on the other hand, that he may reach Girishk before we do, and cross the river, and either fraternize with, or fight and lick the *Wali*, and the outcome of the whole affair will be known at home long before this is received. Whatever happens, the move of the two forces I have mentioned (if men were available) would, I am clear, be the right thing to do, as precautions, at any rate.

As the variety of names that are mentioned in connection with the government of this country are very puzzling, it is well to mention that Abdul Rahman, who stands first for the throne, according to the Mahomedan law of succession, is a first cousin of the deposed *amir*; that Ayoub Khan is the late Amir Yakoob Khan's full brother, and that he comes 2nd, and that the third is the little boy, Musa Jan, who is Jakoob Khan's son. If Abdul Rahman has refused our offers, Ayoub Khan has a good chance, the political officers seem to think, and so he may be coming down here in a friendly manner. However, time will soon show now. This is, I fear, a very dry bit of geography and history, but the first part will be clear enough if read with the map, as then you will see what the moves on the board might be, and, according to my idea, should be.

July 3rd.—Took over command of the Kandahar garrison, and spent the morning in trying, with as much regard to safety as possible, to reduce the guards all over the position, but doing my best the men will be very hardly worked for the present, as will be understood when it is remembered that our infantry are reduced by a whole brigade of 2,000 men. In addition to the two native infantry regiments which will possibly be here within the next fortnight, we hear that the Viceroy has ordered up another complete brigade from the reserve, but it cannot be here for at least six weeks. I cannot myself think this addition necessary, as once we get the 4th and 28th Native Infantry from Quetta; we ought to be fit for anything.

July 4th.—The cavalry brigade, with the battery of horse artillery and company of sappers, marched before daybreak, and starting about an hour after them, and taking a line across country on the excellent Akhbar, who carried me like a bird, I arrived at the first camping ground before the brigade got in. It was a most lovely morning, as we have suddenly gone into quite cool weather, indeed it was quite cold when I started, and the ride was very enjoyable. This change in the weather is extremely pleasant, but of course no one expects it to last and no doubt before the end of the week we shall have it as hot as ever. Still, every cool day is a gain. This sudden change in the aspect of affairs here is remarkable, as ten days ago the idea all over India was, that we should all be on our way back to India in a couple of months, and, instead of that, we are being heavily reinforced, and this would hardly be done if an early retirement was intended. Still so many foolish things have been, and are continually being done, in connection with our campaigns in Afghanistan, that the present moves may mean nothing important after all.

July 5th.—The infantry brigade under General Burrows marched this morning, halting for the day at Kokeran. They did not get off quite so easily and well as the cavalry brigade, as they were hampered by having with them a large quantity of extra ammunition for both rifles and horse artillery guns, and as in this country there is no such thing as a road, and wheeled vehicles of any kind are impossible, everything has to be carried on pack animals, and the trouble and worry of loading and starting has to be seen to be understood.

Here we use five animals for carrying packs—*viz.*, camels, mules, ponies, bullocks, and donkeys, and I should be afraid to say the numbers of each which has accompanied this column. For the extra ammunition alone there were 250 ponies and bullocks, and as in that number there were a certain proportion of bad tempered brutes that at first refused to carry anything at all, delay was inevitable. However, the great comfort in marching is that the first march is always the most tiresome, as each day the men and animals fall more easily into the routine, and in a short time the machine works quite easily. I went out with the brigade to their first halting ground, and having seen them all settled down, rode back to Kandahar, and spent the most of the day in perfecting my arrangements, as far as the means and force at my

disposal would permit, for the safety and protection of our painfully straggling and badly laid out position at Kandahar.

Certainly General Stewart has not left behind him any marks
of a long-seeing and provident general. On the contrary, he
seems to have trusted to good fortune, and fortune seems to
have stuck to him in a remarkable manner. I consider the position here, from a military point of view, bad in all respects, and
that even all the advantage which might have been taken of it
has not been availed of. I have urged my view of the case, and
can do more. As far as one can judge from the appearance of
things, and the reports we get, it is extremely unlikely we should
ever be attacked here, but I don't think that is any reason why
we should not take every precaution. At the same time I must
confess that the weakness of the position has one great advantage, and that is, we should operate in the open, a much better
place for our soldiers than behind walls. I only wish the enemy
would be so badly advised as to attack us, as, with all disadvan-
tages, I have no doubt of the results.

July 6th.—I was up at 4 a.m. and out at half past four, and set
off across country to catch up the brigade and ride a few miles
with them, and then come home. They, however, had started at 4
o'clock also, and so I did not come up with them till they were
twelve miles from Kandahar, which was not to be wondered at,
as they had six miles start of me, and got off half an hour earlier
than I did. I could not, therefore (as I had to be back for breakfast and work), go very much further with them, so, after seeing
them on their way a mile or so further, I struck off through new
country and went straight for camp, which I reached at nine
o'clock. I rode Rufus, who did his twenty-seven miles in first-
class style, and could have done half as many more without any
trouble. The morning was cool, almost cold, and a good deal of
the country very pretty. The climate just now, and the excellent
forage we get, suits the horses very well, and they are all, both
public and private, in first-class order.

July 7th.—Nothing of interest, except that we had news from

Kelat-i-Ghilzi that they had a small skirmish there on the 1st July. The news made me more than ever disappointed that I did not get off to visit that place as was originally intended, as I should then have been in for this affair.

July 8th.—Rode a long way up the Argandab Valley this morning in hopes of picking up some information, or ascertaining if there were any signs of movement or excitement. Everything seemed very quiet, and the people in the numerous villages I rode through were very busy thrashing their corn. An absurd accident happened to me as I was riding home, which at one time threatened, though quite free from any danger to myself, to effect the destruction of my one pair of long riding boots, which would have been an irreparable disaster. I had to ford a small water, channel about six or seven yards wide, the water of which was muddy, but looked quite shallow, so I rode in very carelessly, but had not gone two yards when Mr. Akhbar went right down over his saddle, plunging violently. He managed to get his chest on the bank, and I lost no time in springing on to hard ground and hauling him, with some difficulty, out of the hole, nothing the worse, I am glad to say.

It appears that the people had dug a well about ten feet deep in the bed of the water-course, and it was into this we had got. Of course I was wet through, and so was the saddle, but the sun was warm, and I was an hour and a half from home, and long before I arrived there everything was dry. I had to take my poor boots off most gingerly, and have been nursing them, greatly, and I think they are nothing the worse. I was much more anxious about them than anything else, as nothing of the kind is to be got here, and parcels take two and three months coming up from Bombay. I am beginning to get rather short of clothes, as it was a great loss having all the contents of my portmanteau, which were principally strong warm clothes, looted on the way up here. The orchards of peaches and nectarines in the Argandab Valley are just now quite beautiful to look at. The trees are loaded with most splendid looking fruit, which, however, are rather disappointing when picked, as they don't seem to ripen thoroughly.

July 9th.—We had an unofficial rumour that the advance guard of the *Wali's* army had been met at Washir by the cavalry of Ayoub Khan's army and defeated, but as no confirmation of the rumour has come from General Burrows, we are not inclined to credit it, though it is received as quite true by the people in the city, who are only too glad to believe anything to the detriment of the *Wali*. Of course we must expect all sorts of rumours now, and I am, for curiosity, writing them all down as we get them to see how many eventually prove true, and how many are incorrect.

July 10th.—Today it was reported that considerable disaffection exists among the *Wali's* chiefs and officers, and that the most important man of the lot, the chief of Kokeran, a place about six miles from this, has deserted, and this—July 11th—was so far confirmed that we received official news that he had, with eighty followers, withdrawn himself from the *Wali's* force, although it does not appear, so far, that he has joined Ayoub Khan. In accordance with Afghan customs, the *Wali's* representatives here at once took reprisals by seizing the son of the chief of Kokeran (a small boy in a bad state of health) and putting him in prison, and taking possession of the house and property of the deserter at Kokeran.

July 12th.—Employed during the morning in endeavouring to make arrangements for making the citadel safer and more in accordance with the rules of war, but the task is hopeless, as the place is radically bad in a military point of view, and surrounded with houses on three sides. Strictly speaking these houses should have been knocked down for at least 300 yards all round the wall of the citadel, but General Stewart appears to have set his face against any military precautions, insisting that they were quite unnecessary, "as the people were friendly to us." The consequence is that the whole position here is, strictly speaking, untenable—that is, if an enemy with either organization or means were to come against it. As, however, there is no possibility of any scientific attack being made on us, we feel that, bad as the position is, we can quite engage to hold it, and lick the enemy outside into the bargain. The city of Kandahar is a parallelogram about one and a quarter miles long, and three-quarters of a mile wide, something like this—

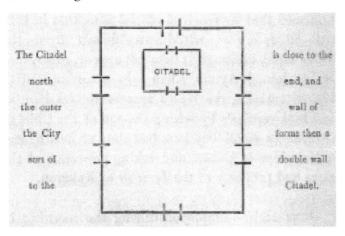

The Citadel is close to the north end, and the outer wall of the City forms then a sort of double wall to the Citadel.

There are six gates in the wall of the city, which is fully twenty to thirty feet high, and very thick and strong.

At each of the city gates there is a guard of native infantry, and we hold the keys of the gates which we lock every night at sunset, after which hour neither entrance nor exit is permitted to anyone. The guards are stationed on the ramparts, and their posts should, from the first, according to the most ordinary rules of war, have been put in a state of defence, but nothing was done to them, and General Primrose has been unwilling to make a change in the matter. Now, however, he has allowed me to take measures to make them safe in the event of any outbreak.

July 13.—A welcome addition to our force reached us today, in the shape of the Head Quarters' wing of the 4th Native Infantry, which marched in from Quetta. The remainder of the regiment will follow shortly. There was a report that Ayoub Khan, with his army, had actually left Furrah, and that his advance guard was at Washir, but there is no confirmation of the collision between his and the *Wali's* forces there, which has probably never occurred. There is much excitement in the city, and the merchants, jewellers, &c, are hiding and burying their property, which means, I assume, that they don't believe in our power to defend the city against Ayoub Khan. A gathering of the enemy is reported as being at Karkrez, about thirty miles off and there is much excitement among the tribes in the Arghastan Valley. There is no doubt it is very desirable that our force at Girishk should have an opportunity of administering a lesson to someone, or we shall probably have to do something in that way ourselves here.

July 14th.—Information received that one of the *Wali's* regiments, composed of men from Kabul, is mutinous. They are in the fort of Girishk with the *Wali*. Ayoub Khan is said to have with him 1,800 cavalry and 4,000 infantry, and thirty guns. So General Burrows' force of 2,500 men and six guns have not much to fear. I visited all the guards on the city gates in the evening, and walked round the whole city on the ramparts, and had a good view of the inhabitants preparing to go to bed on the roofs of their houses, which are flat and always used as the sleeping apartments of the family. The ramparts are twenty to twenty-five feet high, and as the houses are all one-storied, the roofs were much below us, and we saw more of Afghan domestic life than usual, as the people did not anticipate that anyone would be passing round then, and the roofs were covered with ladies, who, however, very quickly let down their veils when they saw us in the distance..

July 15.—News from General Burrows received this morning states, that the whole of the *Wali's* army was mutinous, and that the situation was so critical that he had decided it was necessary he should disregard the positive orders he had received not to cross the Helmund, and that he proposed to do so, and disarm the mutineers. I should explain that our force is, under orders from the Viceroy, halted on the Kandahar side of the Helmund, while the *Wali* and his army are in the fort of Girishk, which is on the Herat side of the Helmund. Later in the day news arrived from the *Wali* (which was apparently authentic), that early the previous morning (14th) the whole of his army left him, taking with them the battery of guns our government had been so idiotic as to give the *Wali*. The letter, which was from the *Wali* to his son, who is here, went on to say, that immediately General Burrows heard this, he had crossed the river with his cavalry and horse artillery, and pursued the mutineers, and coming up with them had killed 200 and recovered the guns.

This report seems authentic, though probably exaggerated, but as yet no confirmation has been received from General Burrows. True or not, the report has had a good effect in the city, and will help to show that the people are not likely to improve matters by trying conclusions with us. I had a deputation from the Parsee shopkeepers, who have followed the army from India, and have shops in our camp, where they sell us wine and provisions, &c, at most exorbitant rates, to beg me to give them a place in the fort for their stores, as they were in a dreadful fright for their lives and their property. Even if I had considered they were in danger, I would not have acceded to their request, as I would much prefer their running certain risks, to giving public confidence the shock of supposing I thought it necessary for our camp followers to take refuge in the fort, so I laughed at their fears, refused their petition, and comforted them by saying, that even if they now lost the whole contents of their shops, they would still be great gainers, as they have made their fortunes already by swindling us.

They did not seem to see this in the light I did, but had to accept the inevitable, and take their share of the risks. As there is a large number of evilly-disposed men in the city, it was decided that it was desirable to show them we were determined to put down any disturbances with a strong hand, so we moved down two of our 40 pounder guns into the fort, and placed them in position to shell the city, and at the same time established a system of strong patrols, which night and day visit the city, and go through all the main streets. There is no denying these patrols would be in an unpleasant position if attacked, as street fighting is, of all, the most disagreeable, but I have given clear and distinct orders for the guidance of the officers in command, from which they learn what they are expected to do, and which will cover their responsibility in resorting, if necessary, to strong measures.

The great objection one feels to returning a fire in a street is, that in such cases it is always unfortunate children and women who suffer, and not the men who deserve it, and who take precious good care to remain under cover. I visited the city myself, and found all quiet, and went with the *Wali's* chief man to arrange for certain improvement to the fortifications, and was quite civilly received everywhere. It was satisfactory to find that already the arrival of the guns in the fort was known and appreciated, and one Afghan said to me, "They" (the guns) "are very big: two discharges from them and the city would be destroyed."

I answered in the language of the country, "I believe you, my boy."

July 16th.—Rode out to Kokeran, and on arrival there, met a well armed caravan, the people composing which could give but an unsatisfactory account of themselves, so one of our native cavalry patrols coming up at the moment, I made the lot prisoners, and sent them into the city to be examined. They may only be peaceful traders armed for their own defence, as they were perfectly civil, but even in that case some information will be got out of them. No news yet from General Burrows, who possibly has gone on in hopes of meeting Ayoub Khan. We have decided to disarm every Afghan approaching Kandahar, and I have issued the necessary orders to ensure this being done.

July 16th.—Rode out to Kokeran in the morning, returning by the Argandab, all seemed quiet. Visited the city in the evening, and found all quiet there also.

July 17th.—Was woke at 2.30 a.m. by the brigade-major bringing the officer commanding the cavalry patrol (which is on duty round the camp all night), who reported that a considerable fire was burning in the direction of Kokeran. As these fires very often indicate a collection of men bent on mischief, I desired him to proceed cautiously with his patrol in the direction of the fire, and ascertain its cause, and bring me information, and at the same time I ordered a troop of cavalry to follow in support. The fire proved to be caused by some evilly-disposed persons having set a light to the corn and straw stacks of a peaceably-disposed native, living some eight or nine miles from camp, and the patrol found no signs of a gathering of men, so returned to camp. Confirmation was received from General Burrows of his successful fight at Girishk against our supposed friends, the troops of the *Wali*, in which he had succeeded in recovering the battery of artillery which our Government had given as a present to the *Wali*, and the first time it was used was to fire upon us! General Burrows also recovered a great deal of stores and baggage belonging to the *Wali*, and much ammunition, and on the whole made a very successful business, losing but very few men himself, the loss of the enemy being computed by themselves at 400, but was probably not more than half that number.

There being a want of supplies at Girishk, General Burrows thought it right to fall back to a place twenty-five miles nearer to Kandahar, called Kushki-Nakud. There were many good reasons, I confess, for this move, but personally I would never willingly, in Eastern warfare, take a retrograde step, except under the strongest compulsion, as Afghans know nothing, and care less, about the laws of strategy, and see only defeat in any but forward movements. The fact is, had we known that the *Wali's* army intended to mutiny, we would never have advanced beyond Kushki-Nakud, as there are many good objections to the position at Girishk.

That we did not know the shaky state of the *Wali's* troops is all the fault of the Political officer with the *Wali*, who, wishing to see all things *couleur de rose,* persuaded himself that all was right, and could not, or would not, believe any evil of them. Even he must now see what we have felt sure of all along, that Shere Ali is quite without power or influence, and quite unable to maintain his own authority for a day without our assistance. We have, of course, here, the reflex of the events at Girishk, as there has been a very marked increase of excitement and turbulence in the city, since the news of the mutiny of the *Wali's* troops has arrived, and had not, at the same time, the intelligence of the licking they had received from us reached the city, we should certainly have had an outbreak there.

July 18th.—Moved another 40 pounder gun into the fort, and mounted it on a very commanding position, from which we could soon destroy the best part of the city. Of course there is no intention of a measure of this kind, but a big gun ready for action has a very soothing effect on the warlike feelings of Afghans, or Easterns generally. Intelligence was brought in, that attacks on the posts of Mandi Hissar and Abdul Rahmon were likely, and though it was not thought there was much chance of these places, which are now very fairly strong, being attacked, it was thought wise to send some cavalry to reconnoitre, which was done; but the officer, on arrival at Abdul Rahmon (twenty-five miles off), was able to telegraph that all was quiet and no sign of gatherings or excitement. If, however, the existing state of feeling in the country grows or becomes intensified, it is quite possible these posts may be attacked, but if so they should be well able to hold their own.

July 19th.—Was suddenly woke at 2 a.m. by the sound of a volley of musketry close to our quarters, followed by the noise of horses galloping. I at once recognised what had happened—indeed it was the only thing which could have happened—that the cavalry patrol had been fired on by some of the enemy. I lost no time in getting to the best place for a view, and presently one of the patrols rode up and reported that as they had been passing along, about 200 yards from our quarters, a volley had been fired into them from behind a low wall, and that several men and horses had been hit. I immediately sent off orders for two companies of the 7th Fusiliers and a troop of cavalry to turn out, and getting dressed as quickly as possible, was mounted and ready before the troops could come. We then carefully swept the whole ground round the camp, but of course failed to find the attackers, although we certainly were on their track ten minutes after they had fired. The country round our camp lends itself in the most unsatisfactory manner to small attacks of this kind, as on all sides there are enormous cemeteries, with thousands of graves and vaults, into any of which a few men could get and hide with absolute safety. The night was dark, the moon having set, and a haze come up, as it generally does here towards morning.

On investigation I found that the native officer commanding the patrol was badly wounded in the arm, and that two horses were slightly wounded, and one soldier and one horse were killed. While I and the brigade-major, and the cavalry colonel, were standing together, near the man who was killed, an intelligent (?) native sentry who was posted about 400 yards off, took it into his wise head to decide that we were a party of the enemy, and putting a bullet into his rifle, took a deliberate and, I must say, extremely good shot at us, aiming, I am glad to say, just a few feet too high. I had not heard the whiz of a rifle bullet since the China days, but I had no difficulty in recognizing it again, and as soon as weightier matters allowed, I had my friend, the sentry, made a prisoner of, and properly punished the next morning.

All things considered, we have had very little wild firing by sentries here, but, as is always the case; there have been some few instances which I have not failed to punish without accepting any excuses. This little affair of the patrol is another excellent instance of how little Sir Donald Stewart did to make the position here as good in a military sense as it could be—as had he done so, he would not have left a wall or enclosure standing within a thousand yards of our camp anywhere. He, however, would have none of them touched, first because he wanted to conciliate the people; and next, because he wanted to save the expense of pulling them down. When General Primrose came he accepted the existing state of affairs, and would allow nothing to be done, although General Burrows and I naturally have wished to have things more ship-shape.

I lost no time in pointing a moral, and adorning a tale after the affair of the patrol, and got permission to take down all walls and enclosures in the immediate vicinity of the Barracks, of which permission I have availed myself to the full, and a little over, and made a very perceptible improvement, though I am by no means contented yet. I asked General Primrose to insist on the "*Wali's* people levelling various big enclosures between our position and the city walls, but as they surround very holy shrines and mosques, they begged for a respite on promise of good behaviour, and I am sorry to say it has been granted. However, what has been done is most useful, and makes the work of the patrols easier and safer. It was very unfortunate that the native officer commanding the patrol should have been shot in the right arm, and his horse wounded, as he was unable to pull up the horse for some distance, and so did not succeed in seeing where the men who attacked him went to.

July 20th.—Paid my usual visit to the city, and found all very quiet, and the people by no means uncivil. In the evening I took all the cavalry officers, English and native, round the camp, and gave them my ideas of the way in which they should patrol, and what a patrol should do when fired on *(i.e., not run away).*

July 21.—Having arranged with Major Adam, the assistant quartermaster-general, to make a reconnaissance through the villages in the Argandab, we started from camp at half-past 4 o'clock (a lovely fresh morning), and, crossing the Baba-i-Wali Pass, rode for several miles up the valley as far as a village called Sardeh Bala.—(N.B.—You will find all these places on the big map I sent you last mail, which will give you a capital idea of the events I have now to tell of). Turning back from there we proposed to return into the Kandahar plain by the pass across the range of hills (which separates the plain from the Argandab Valley) which is called the Kotal-i-Murcha. This range of hills, which is very clearly marked on the big map, rises to a considerable height, being often as much as 2,000 to 2,500 feet above the plain. The two passes through the range are the Baba-i-Wali and the Kotal-i-Murcha.

The first is passable by men and horses, and we have made a road for guns over it. The second is a mere mountain track, up which not more than one man can go abreast, and part of which is so strewn with detached rocks that it is absolutely necessary to dismount and lead a horse along it. This pass, however, is a short cut from the city into the Argandab, and we have all used it regularly when riding out there. I myself rode that way on the 16th, and there was, therefore, nothing rash or unwise in our returning that way. From the commencement of the ascent to the top of the pass is about half a mile, and the rise in that distance is 700 to 800 feet and therefore very steep. We had just commenced the ascent when one of our escorts drew our attention to some men dodging behind the rocks over our head, who had guns, and were evidently trying to avoid being seen.

An armed man is so usual a sight in this country that I did not for the moment think anything of the matter, and indeed prevented Major Adam, who said he would like to take a shot at the nearest man from doing so. As a precaution, however, I ordered three of the escort to dismount and get out their carbines, and Major Adam took a carbine, and so did I, and we slowly ascended, keeping our eye on our friends, or rather on the place they had been, for we could not see them then. Presently (all this occurred in less time than I write it) we saw one scoundrel pop his head up from behind a stone and take aim. We were too quick for him, for Major Adam and one of the escort let fly at him, and so threw out his aim, that he fired high, and no one was touched. Immediately, however, three more shots were fired, one killing one of the horses of the escort, our fire in return being quite harmless, as our assailants were behind rocks, and we were out in the open. Still it served to unsteady their aim, and we got to the top and under cover without further damage, though most of the shots had been fairly well directed for us.

I had one shot as I came up, which, I am sorry to say, was not successful, though I made my friend "leave that," as Paddy Roe used to say when I fired at a hare and, according to my custom, missed it. As soon as I got the party under cover I sent men down on each side of the hill (having first sent off to Kandahar, four and a half miles off, for twenty infantry to help in the hunt through the rocks) to prevent the enemy getting down and running away, and Major Adam and I, each with two men and a pocketful of ammunition, essayed climbing the hill. He first descended a good bit and hit off a fairish path which took him a long way up, and during the ascent he had four or five shots, but never could get near the fellows at all, they being all mountaineers, and we being burdened with heavy riding boots, spurs, &c, and knowing nothing of the paths.

I, with my two men, made excellent progress at first, but found ourselves regularly stuck on the top of a precipice, across which, at about 300 yards, we could see one of the men making off. I took, as I thought, very good aim, making one of the men with me fire too, but we again missed, whereupon the runaway turned round and let fly at us, but expecting this we were safely behind a rock, and I don't think his bullet came near us. I had then to descend, and before I could hit off another path, the whole lot were out of sight. It was dreadfully hot, and we were dying of thirst, and not a drop of water within three miles, but of course had to stay until the infantry came. I sent off one of my two men to Kandahar with news to tell them the direction the enemy had run in, and I and the other man comfortably behind a good rock with our carbines ready, waited in hopes of getting a better shot, but never saw our assailants again. In due course first some cavalry, and then, after a considerable interval, some infantry came out to me, and we hunted the hill, but it was so precipitous and so full of caves that our search was without result.

I did not, of course, accompany this party as I wanted to get back to camp, and besides was nearly dead with thirst. I cannot, I fear, give a good idea of the difficulties of climbing or searching this range of hills which are nothing but limestone rocks, not a tree, blade of grass, or inch of earth on them, so one might as well be trying to climb the cliffs at Bundoran, only that these hills are much higher. I dare say you will think it was a good deal of trouble and time to spend over a small party of marauders of this kind, and so it was, but my reason was that I was anxious to impress by practice what I have so often preached, the necessity for officers and men on such occasions as this always trying to give as good as they get, and not considering they had done their duty when they followed the example of Captain Carey and others by galloping away as fast as they could.

With this object in view, I don't think I was wrong to turn myself for an hour or so into a private soldier, and do a little skirmishing on foot with a carbine. We had eight men of the native cavalry with us, and they were as staunch as steel and very quiet and cool, except the two men who I sent into Kandahar with the order to send me out help, which order I wrote, and in a most guarded way, saying "I want twenty infantry, and a few cavalry as scouts." However, once away from the influence of the officers, the imagination of my orderlies magnified the whole affair, and as they rode through the camp they told everyone that the general *sahib* had been fired at and was engaged in a great battle with thousands of the enemy who were pressing on to Kandahar. This, unfortunately, was believed, and all the troops were turned out, and a regular commotion got up in the city, and altogether a very objectionable state of alarm was arrived at.

When I came in and heard of it, I gave all concerned a lecture which they won't forget, for if there is one thing I hate more than another it is false alarms, and so far I have not had one. And now I must defend myself against the idea everyone seems to have that I go about here rashly, as I really do not, as I always have my escort, and till the last ten days it was quite safe to move about, and in this particular instance it never for a moment entered Major Adam's or my mind that there was the slightest risk going over the Murcha Pass. Had we thought so we would have avoided it, but once being in the business there was only one thing for us to do, and that was to see it through. Lots of men, women, and children had crossed the pass that morning, and we had met them and spoken to them.

My rides are now much circumscribed, and I don't think just at present of going any distance from camp merely for amusement. Yesterday we went on business, and with what is considered, and what proved to be, a quite sufficient escort. I was riding my white horse, Selim, and he behaved like an angel, and took no notice of the firing, and when I had to dismount at the bad piece of the pass, followed me up without any difficulty. Afterwards I fastened him to a stone, and he stood quite quietly there for four hours without giving any trouble. I did not get in till half past one, very thirsty, very hungry, and very hot, but this kind of work never does me any harm, and I was as fit as possible as soon as I had a bath and my breakfast.

July 22nd.—Heard from the government of India that Abdul Rahman is to be proclaimed *Amir* of Kabul forthwith by Sir D. Stewart. I cannot think this a wise step, but the desire to get out of the war at any cost is, I think, blinding the government to the many weak points in the arrangement.

July 23rd.—Visited the city in order that I might give General Primrose my views of an idea of his to occupy a certain portion of it without troops should we be attacked here. The arrangement does not seem to me to be either necessary or desirable, as I would prefer keeping all our small force, except the garrison of the fort and the city walls, in the open, striking at the enemy whenever opportunity offered. I have explained this, and I hope it will, if necessity arise, be carried out. When riding to the Fort this morning I was stopped by a native who informed me he had something very important to tell me, which was, that this being the Mahomedan Sunday (Friday) a rising was to take place today. The old gentleman, who belonged to the Moghul or Persian tribe, who hate the Afghans, was in an awful fright, and I think he allowed his fears to magnify matters much. However, I am keeping my eyes open, have taken all precautions, and am ready, but fear the Afghans won't come to the point.

July 24th.—The guard on the Shikarpore Gate of the city

was fired on by some armed men during the night, the fire being returned by the guard. In reporting the matter to General Primrose, I strongly urged that the walls and buildings outside the city gates, which afforded cover to villains of sorts to approach and fire at our guards, should be demolished. This, however, would have involved much distress and annoyance to the Afghans, and he did not care to push the matter strongly (after events, however, proved that the suggestion was a proper one). We received news that 150 of our cavalry, under General Nuttall, had completely routed 600 of Ayoob Khan's Cavalry.

July 25th.—Three companies of the 28th Native Infantry arrived from Chaman, a most welcome addition, small as it is, to our painfully weak force.

July 26th.—The guard on the Herat Gate was fired on during the early morning. I again urged the necessity for demolishing all cover near the gates, but the measure was deemed too strong. I am determined, if possible, to catch the scoundrels who go about, and hold parties of cavalry and infantry in readiness all night to go without delay to any place where firing of this desultory nature is heard. This is harassing to the troops, but cannot be helped. Two more companies of the 28th Native Infantry arrived.

July 27th.—I got information that some of the enemy were concealed in the hills above old Kandahar, so, obtaining permission from General Primrose to make a raid on them, I despatched parties of the 7th Fusiliers and 4th Native Infantry to see if the report was correct, and if so to attack and defeat them. I rode out myself in the afternoon to see how the search through the very difficult ground was being carried on, and quite approved the arrangements made by Major Marshall who was in command. No one, however, was found, though there were evident signs that several places had been recently inhabited, and very hurriedly evacuated.

July 28th.—I was woke at 1.30 a.m. by Colonel La Touche, of the cavalry, who came to report to me that a small portion (a native officer and thirty men) of one of the cavalry regiments with General Burrows' force had just reached camp, having, they said, rode sixty miles without drawing rein to bring the information of the total annihilation, by Ayoob Khan's army, of the force under General Burrows. They declared that a great battle had been fought the previous day about noon; that after holding out for five hours under a terrible fire, that the whole force had been broken up and taken to flight, and been cut to pieces in detail. Both Generals, Burrows and Nuttall, were said to be dead, that no one, but these men themselves, was saved.

The story was a terrible one, and enough to shock the stoutest heart and nerves. I could not, and would not, believe it in its entirety, and told Colonel La Touche that I felt sure things were not as black as they were painted, though I feared they were bad enough. The first thing, however, was to take the news to General Primrose, so, pulling on a few clothes, I ran over to his house with Colonel La Touche and told him the bad news, at the same time recommending caution in accepting, without some reserve, the story of the native officer and men of the Sind Horse.

A disaster had, without doubt, occurred, and the only question was whether or not a remnant had escaped, and if so of what strength. A hurried consultation was held, and it was unanimously agreed that, with the certainty of the whole country rising like one man against us, it would be worse than madness for our small force to attempt to hold the altogether indefensible military position which the parsimony and want of military forethought on the part of Sir Donald Stewart had bequeathed to us. As I have often remarked hitherto on the hopeless position, from a military point of view, of the Kandahar cantonments, it is useless repeating all the objections to them again. Suffice it to say, that they have no independent water supply; that they are commanded on one side by two low hills, and that they are straggling, and entirely without military defences of any kind, and that no amount of labour or money could have made them tenable in the few days at our disposal.

Our only alternative was to accept another utterly false military position, and to occupy the whole city of Kandahar, it being impossible to place our force, small as it was, in the citadel, nor (could we have done so) to have held the citadel against an enemy in possession of the city. It is hardly necessary to point out the dangers in, and objections to, the occupation of the city, as they are self-evident, the first and chief one being the vastness of its size in comparison with the force at our disposal. The city, of which I give a rough plan on one of the foregoing pages, is a sort of irregular parallelogram, one side (N.) being 1,200 yards long; the W. 1,900 yards long, the S. 1,300 yards long, and the E. 2,000 yards long, a total length of wall of something under four miles, to protect which, and an additional half mile of wall in the citadel, we should have, unless some portion of General Burrows' force returned, not quite 1,500 men.

When I mention that to defend lines of this length, according to military rules, a force of 18,000 men is considered the correct thing—the almost hopelessness of the position may be imagined. Behind and within these walls lay a city with a population of 30,000, of whom 14,000 were men, out of whom it was no exaggeration to feel that half at least must of necessity be our deadly enemies, and that consequently, in addition to offering resistance to hordes without, we had to guard against treachery from within. The position, for these two reasons alone, was utterly wrong, but it was the sole possible alternative, and had to be accepted, and its difficulties and dangers dealt with as might be possible. The question of water was the urgent one, but as we knew the city had a sufficient supply for its inhabitants, of which we purposed to turn out at least one half, we trusted we should get enough for ourselves.

The walls vary in height from eighteen feet in the lowest place to twenty-five feet in the highest, and are about twenty feet thick at the base, and twelve to fourteen feet broad at the parapet. There are six gates—four principal ones— from which the various faces take their names, and two minor ones. The northern gate is called the Eedgah; the southern the Shikarpore, being the gate from which the main road to India leads; the western gate is the Kabul gate, and near it a smaller one known as the Bar Dourani; the eastern gate is the Herat gate, and close to it another called the Topkhana or artillery gate. Along the walls, at intervals of hundred yards, are high turrets, which give the only flanking defence, very poor in quality and degree. This point hurriedly, but definitely and decidedly, settled, we had no time for conversation or consideration, as immediate action was necessary, the carrying out of which General Primrose placed unreservedly in my hands.

The first thing to be done was to have the sick and ammunition conveyed to a place of safety in the citadel, and as it was clear we could not use our heavy battery (*viz.*, four 40-pounders and two six-inch mortars), drawn by bullocks in the field, I sent it also without delay into the citadel, and issued orders to all commanding officers to move all public and private property belonging to their regiments to the citadel also. About 4 a.m. one or two. native stragglers from General Burrows' force came in and gave a less terrible account of the destruction which had befallen it than the Sind Horse had done, and at quarter to 5 a.m. Veterinary-Surgeon Oliver, of the horse artillery, arrived and was brought to me. He was greatly exhausted, but I learned from him that there was a very considerable proportion of the force saved, and that the main body was covering the retreat, and was probably then about ten miles off, Generals Burrows and Nuttall being with them.

I sent Mr. Oliver on to General Primrose, who had ridden down to the citadel to start work there, to tell his story, and convey a message from me that I requested permission to take a small force and move out in the direction of Kokeran to cover General Burrows' retirement. Feeling sure the proposal would be approved, I ordered

1 troop of cavalry,
2 guns,
4 companies of infantry

to be held in readiness to march at once. About three quarters of an hour later General Primrose arrived from the citadel and authorized my starting at once, urging on me, however, to use great caution, and avoid, as far as possible, any considerable loss of life. Being anxious to be off at once, I had no time to give any attention to getting my own property into the citadel, but had to leave the matter to my native servant, telling him to do the best he could, and to take the most useful things into safety first, and I may here say that he must have worked admirably, as, when I got to the fort at 7 o'clock in the evening, I found he had brought off in safety every single thing I possessed. At half past 5 o'clock (three quarters of an hour after I first heard that any remnants of Burrows' force was saved, and trying to return) I paraded my little force, which was, I was horrified to find, much smaller than I had intended, as the full number of men were not at the moment available. Time was precious to our poor comrades wearily fighting their way back to camp, so I decided not to wait till I could get my numbers, and started with only

40 Sabres native cavalry,
2 Guns R. A.,
70 of the 7th Fusiliers.
100 of the 28th Native Infantry,

I knew there could be no organized resistance, and that if I was cautious I could come to no harm, but, all the same, I am free to confess that I could not avoid feeling anxious about my guns, as the loss of two more would have been simply ruin to us. I must here describe the route I had to follow, as its peculiarities added much to the difficulties and dangers of the enterprise. Immediately after leaving the barracks the road passes for about half a mile through walled gardens, each garden forming a little fortification of itself, and giving cover for any number of armed men. These passed through, the village of Abasabad is reached through the main street of which the road goes.

This street is so narrow that in places it was a close shave to get the R.A. carriages through, and it twists and winds about most unpleasantly.

Beyond the village is another quarter of a mile of walled gardens, and then an open plain is come to with, however, commanding hills all along the road to the right (about 300 yards off), and on the left a string of strongly placed villages about the same distance from the road. It is evident, therefore, that every inch of road offered extraordinary facilities for the enemy to resist our advance.

As we left the camp we began to meet the first of the long string of fugitives, who continued afterwards to pass us till we reached Kokeran, a more terrible sight I never witnessed; all appearance of organization or discipline gone; each man, whether European or native, was fighting, as it were, for his own life, careful of nothing but getting into safety. All were wearied and harassed, and many unable hardly to move one foot before the other, as indeed was not wonderful, considering that since 4 p.m. the previous day they had been marching, with a cruel enemy on all sides of them, shooting and stabbing every man who, too wearied to drag on, sat down for a moment's rest.

To add to the horrors of the march they had, in the whole distance of over fifty miles, found water only twice, and what this means no one who has not lived and worked in this climate can tell. From all I can hear there were some marvellous instances of self-denial in this matter: men giving up their last drop of water, which was more than their lives to them, to men more feeble than themselves, and, apparently, none equalled or exceeded in this respect Captain Slade, of the horse artillery, as noble a soldier as ever lived.

Officers and men have since told me of his heroic efforts to save his guns, to give assistance and to sacrifice his life, or deny himself to save or help anyone; all also join in saying General Burrows' conduct was splendid, and that he had fairly won the Victoria Cross three or four times.

Once when all hope seemed lost, for dismounted men he got off his horse, put two wounded officers on it, and led it himself for three miles, with a howling crowd of savages following him, anxious for his life. I had never seen the retreat of a panic-stricken military force before, and I trust I never may do so again, as it is too horrible for description, and this retreat excelled in terror any that I have ever read of. As each inch of the road (till my little force was seen) had to be fought for against a set of blood-thirsty savages, rather than fall into whose hands alive, it is said several men shot themselves, knowing the horrible fate that would otherwise be in store for them. Then the want of water was a fearful aggravation of the sufferings of the wretched men, and the length of the march, fifty miles, made the hope of escape seem impossible.

I must now go back to my own enterprise, which, I rejoice to think, was successful, and resulted in the saving of many valuable lives. I had hardly got my little force in column of route outside the barrack gates, when the enemy commenced a desultory and harmless fire on us from behind the walls of the neighbouring gardens. I at once sent forward some skirmishers to the front, and a cavalry piquet to the extreme right and left, and was glad to see the spirit with which all advanced, which at once told on the rabble opposed to us, who gave up their positions and ran for their lives, several being killed as they ran. In this way, pressing on steadily, I cleared the gardens and the village of Abasabad, and was able to bring my guns and remainder of my column through that extremely awkward position.

On the other side of the village the skirmishers had advanced, driving the enemy before them, till the more open ground was reached. Here I formed up my column once more, preparatory to pushing on for Kokeran. On the range of high hills which ran along the left of the road, at about 300 yards off, were small bodies of the enemy, as also in the strongly placed villages on my left. Before advancing I had to send out small parties on either flank to dislodge these people, which they did with the greatest ease. My way was again clear, and I advanced without opposition for about a mile, when, on a low hill, about 2,000 yards to my right front, I saw a considerable force posted, which was being increased every moment by contingents from the villages in the rear of the hill, from which we could see people hurrying in great numbers. Seeing a good position about 1,000 yards ahead, I pushed on to it rapidly, and getting my guns into action, threw forward the cavalry to threaten the left flank, while the infantry moved slowly to the front.

A couple of shells planted, with charming precision, by my friend Captain Law had a most happy effect, and, as we could see, shook the confidence of the enemy, good as their position was. They did not, however, seem disposed to take the hint, and kept up a constant, but, owing to the distance, harmless fire on us as we advanced. Presently, however, on a repetition of the dose equally well administered, assisted by a few volleys from our rifles, they broke, the greater part rushing to the rear, but some, as I had hoped, trying to cross the road and gain the shelter of the hills on the left. This was the moment for the cavalry, who charged with excellent effect, doing good execution at the same time. I gave the fugitives to the rear a couple of shells at 2,000 yards where, thinking themselves safe, they had halted to breathe.

Serious as the work on hand was, we could not help a hearty laugh at the consternation caused by the unexpected visitors. The mass of people broke away in all directions, leaving, as we could see afterwards as we advanced, a good percentage on the ground. I dare say there are some critics who will think that this position ought to have been carried at the point of the bayonet, in order that a severe lesson might have been inflicted, and under other circumstances I might have thought so myself, but, placed as we were when the loss of every man was serious, I had determined to utilize to the utmost the long range of our weapons, and to do all the fighting I could at long bowls, and by sticking steadily to this, I succeeded in carrying out my object which entailed a march of fourteen miles, every inch of which had to be contested or defended, with the loss only of one man killed and two or three slightly wounded. I quite acknowledge there are objections to the arrangement, but I feel sure it was the right one for the occasion.

After this no regular opposition was offered till I reached Kokeran, which is a large village with a fortified enclosure in its midst, which was full of the enemy, who had been ill treating the stragglers of General Burrows' force all morning. Knowing the ground well, I at once selected my position, and was quickly placed to command the whole of the country round. I was just going to give the order for the guns to come into action, when, to my delight, at about a mile off, at the spot where I knew was the ford of the Argandab, where the road from Girishk crossed the river, I saw a mass of men which I at once recognized as what remained of General Burrows' force. I decided, therefore, before hammering Kokeran to communicate with them, and sent some cavalry to make a circuit to the right and join General Burrows, informing him that I was clearing his way, and that he might, I felt sure, advance in twenty minutes, by which time I would have his way open. The cavalry had hardly started before I recognized that the enemy, seeing that the position I had taken up had rendered Kokeran untenable, had suddenly evacuated that place, and taken up an extremely strong position on my right flank, from which, without delay, they opened a heavy fire on us. A few shells and a rapid demonstration, for it never reached a hand-to-hand fight, soon, however, did their business, and, to my great satisfaction, I found myself able to ask General Burrows to come on along a perfectly safe road.

It was a sad cavalcade, many wounded, all well nigh tired to death. The gun carriages, alas, reduced by two, which had been lost, covered with sick, wounded, dead and dying, while the wretched horses, dying themselves of thirst and fatigue, were hardly able to drag them along. Many poor fellows, wounded almost to death, trying with a terrible anxiety to cling to the back of a horse or a camel, knowing too well the fate that would await them if they failed to keep their seats. To these latter my appearance was a double blessing, as I had brought with me twenty-five litters (*palanquins*), into which the worst cases were placed, and they were able to finish their journey in comparative comfort.

One poor fellow (Major Iredell) had a compound fracture of the ankle, and his foot was merely hanging on by the skin, and yet he had ridden for eighteen hours, and was wonderfully well, and is, I hope, now in a fair way to recovery. Almost last of all, followed only by a cavalry escort, came poor Burrows himself, who, poor fellow, completely broke down when he saw me, and could not say a word. I made him get off his horse and take a little whiskey and water I had with me, and a bit of biscuit, and soon he was more composed and better. He, like them all, was relieved beyond measure to see me, and my diminutive following, as they knew their troubles were at an end. I agreed that they should all, to the last straggler, pass me, and that when they were half a mile ahead I should follow slowly, and bring up the rear of all, covering them from all annoyance.

Soon (all too soon, for they were but a very little company) they had filed passed, and I then recalled my cavalry, which had been watching the ford of the Argandab a mile to my front. On their return over this mile the enemy, emboldened by our preparations for departure, suddenly rushed down in great numbers to cut them off, but Captain Anderson was equal to the occasion, and setting at nought the difference of numbers, charged them, and cut his way through, leaving, however, his very best soldier dead on the ground. Although I would have liked to have punished the enemy for this affair, prudence said no, and so I commenced my return for Kandahar, keeping half a mile in rear of General Burrows' column, and picking up many poor fellows (putting them on my guns), who, even in this short distance, had begun to fall out again. For the first three miles after leaving Kokeran, all was absolute quiet, the result of the lessons of the morning, and the wearied column from Girishk passed along in unaccustomed peace.

At this time, however, I received information from the front, that the enemy had collected in great force on the hills. around and in the village of Abasabad, and that help to turn them out was wanted. I immediately hurried my guns and cavalry to the front, and followed on with the Infantry, desiring Captain Law to pass General Burrows' force, and getting to his front open fire on the enemy. This he did in good style, and was making an advance to a second position, when I and the infantry, who had also passed through General Burrows' force, which were halted, came up. We completed the dispersion of the enemy with artillery fire, and then throwing out skirmishers swept, for a second time that day, the gardens round Abasabad.

This accomplished, and the road again clear for General Burrows' force, I formed up on one flank and allowed them again to pass me, following them into the cantonments, which I reached about half past one or two o'clock, very thankful indeed that I had gone out, and but little less delighted that I had managed to effect my object at such a very small loss. To ensure a safe conduct to any unfortunate straggler that might, by accident, have escaped notice, I sent a fresh company of the 7th Regiment to hold the entrance to the village of Abasabad, and kept them there till all hopes of anyone coming in had gone, when I withdrew them. My column had constantly been on the move from half-past 5 a.m. till half-past one p.m., the most of the time under a burning sun, which made us all, even those who were riding, suffer from an intolerable thirst, and as there was no water between Kokeran and Kandahar, this was a great addition to our labours.

On arrival in cantonments General Burrows' force received orders to pass on to the citadel, while I was desired to take in hands, without delay, measures for the evacuation of the cantonments, and the safe conduct of all the troops there into the citadel. The operation was most distasteful, but I had agreed to the necessity for it, and quite saw it was the only possible course. When I came to enquire into the position of affairs I was horrified to find that the eight precious hours while I had been absent had been wasted in the most inexplicable way. Apparently little or nothing of the government or private property in charge of regiments had been moved to the fort, and all had yet to be done. It was then past 2 o'clock, and General Primrose telegraphed to me from the citadel, to say he wished me to move in there as quickly as possible. (I ought to explain that the citadel or fort of Kandahar is about one and a quarter miles from the cantonments.) I at once set everyone to work, excusing no one and superintending all personally, to get as much property as possible into the fort, sending there for all available carts, camels, ponies and mules, each of which, immediately it had got rid of its load, came back again, and so the afternoon passed away all too rapidly.

At last all was safely sent in, except the baggage of the 66th, which was one of the regiments of General Burrows' brigade, who, when going out to Girishk, had left some tons of things in a most careless and unpacked condition. I saw it would be hopeless had I had a day instead of an hour to get all in, but I put on big working parties, and worked away, putting off my departure from half hour to half hour, until it approached 6 o'clock, and I had been called on three or four times by General Primrose to move into the citadel. I then saw it was useless to try and save more, and so I fixed quarter past 6 o'clock as the hour for our departure, deciding that all not packed then must be abandoned. All this time I had been pressed all round by marauding bands of armed men, who were sweeping round, trying to kill and steal who and what they could. These necessitated strong picquets, and, from time to time, small expeditions, so my hands were full. At quarter past six I paraded my force as follows:—

4th Native Infantry,
28th Native Infantry,
C/2 Royal Artillery,
7th Fusiliers,
Poona Horse,
Detachment 3rd Light Cavalry,
    "   "   3rd Sind Horse,

and in this order commenced my mournful and humiliating march. I had previously gone carefully round the whole place myself, had had it carefully searched by an officer with a piquet, and had made each commanding officer and the chief medical officer report to me that nothing was left behind. At the moment I marched I withdrew my picquets and guards, and covering my rear with cavalry, moved on the fort. When every man had left the large barrack square I returned to it myself and made my staff and escort, who were with me, pass out before me, so that I might have the melancholy satisfaction of being the last man in the place.

At 7 p.m. I followed the last man of the force into the citadel and shut the gates, and so began a fresh act of this extremely painful drama. With the exception of a portion of the clothing of the 66th Regiment, I had succeeded in getting the property of the regiments which were under me into safety, but I fear much, owing to some mismanagement, I am inclined almost to fear a panic, after we had started for Kokeran, several of the regiments hurriedly and unnecessarily evacuated their barracks early in the morning, when they were at once entered by the enemy and plundered.

On starting, I made over the command to the next senior officer, giving him distinct instructions how to act, but as he himself lost some of the baggage of his regiment (in my absence), he cannot have paid much attention to them. Late as it was when I entered the citadel, my work was not yet done, as I was the only general officer available to issue orders or do work, as General Primrose, who was seedy, was thoroughly wearied out, and Generals Burrows and Nuttall were sound asleep, and poor fellows badly they needed it after the terrible night they had gone through. I had, therefore, to set to work to put the guards and necessary defences for the night in some state of order, and as this involved a walk and ride round the city and fort walls, four and a half miles, it was a pleasant ending to a long day.

At 8 o'clock I snatched a hurried dinner with General Primrose, the first food, except a cup of chocolate and a biscuit, I had had in the day, and at half-past nine went the round of the ramparts and guards, getting to bed at 1 a.m., having had twenty-three and a half hours of intense work of mind and body, eighteen of which I had spent in the saddle. I did not want much rocking, and was horrified to find, long before I was half satisfied with sleep, that it was 5 a.m. on the 29th July, and that I had to get up to start off a reconnoitring party of cavalry to ascertain the state of affairs round our old cantonments. They found the whole country covered with armed men, and the cantonment looted, and such parts of it as would burn, burned down. They were fired on at several places, but returned unopposed to camp.

We were hard at work all day, improving our defences and removing the cover which surrounded the outside of the gates, but it was clear this, was, with our small force, the work of many days, and that if we were soon attacked we would have to make the best of things as they were. In the afternoon the enemy's cavalry appeared in large numbers on our left front. We immediately turned out our cavalry brigade, who, however, could not get near the enemy's, as they retired under the shelter of their guns, where we did not care to follow them. The night passed quite quietly, there being strong guards on all the walls, and everyone sleeping in their clothes, ready to turn out at a moment's notice.

It is necessary I should mention that on the previous day, while I was at Kokeran, General Primrose was busy in the city, seizing on all the principal parts, closing and securing the gates, and keeping the inhabitants overawed—all works, any failure in which would have been utter destruction to us. On the morning of the 28th, therefore, our small force had three important duties to perform: 1st, to go out and assist the retiring column; 2nd, to seize and hold the city, and fortify it, and prepare for the siege; 3rd, to hold the cantonments—any one of them a task quite sufficient for the strength of the Force, so that our accomplishing all three was a matter of great satisfaction.

July 30.—Sent out a reconnoitring party of cavalry, and directed the officer so to approach the enemy's camp as to try and draw him out, which he did very successfully, giving us an excellent opportunity of treating him with good effect to a few shells. General Burrows and I urged on General Primrose the absolute necessity for turning out of the city the whole of the Pathans, and he authorized us to go to the political officer and the *Wali*, and urge the great importance of this matter, and notify his determination to have it carried out. A little explanation on this subject is necessary. The population of the city of Kandahar is made up of three sections, the largest of which are Pathans, who are all Orthodox Mahomedans, very bitter against all foreigners or infidels, and our irreconcilable enemies. The next are the Moghuls or Parsiwans, who, though Mahomedans, are accounted a species of dissenter by the true Mahomedans, and hated and persecuted by them accordingly. Their sympathies are therefore (speaking comparatively) with us.

The third and last are the Hindoo Merchants, an influential and numerous community, settlers from India, intent only on making money, despised by both sects of Mahomedans, who, in turn, prey on them and rob them. They are quite valueless as friends or foes, but such as they were their feelings are with us. The Pathans, to a man, were our enemies, and their presence in the city our deadliest danger, and it, seemed to me quite useless to fortify our position or take measures against the enemy without, if we wilfully permitted a base and treacherous foe to remain within, our walls.

The measure of turning out many innocent people was a hard and painful one, but it was one on which our very existence rested, and so I was most urgent on the point. As I expected, the political officers objected, and tried to persuade us that the risk was imaginary, &c. However, I was firm, and after a long and hot conversation which, at one time, seemed likely to culminate in a row, I carried the day, and an order was issued that all Pathans (men) should leave the city, and that in the afternoon search parties would go round to ascertain that the order was being obeyed.

This unpleasant duty was confided to me, and I made all preparations for resistance, but in no case met with any, and it was clear the exodus had commenced, and eventually resulted in about 12,000 persons leaving the city of their own free will.

This was a gain not only in getting rid of a certain set of desperate enemies, but also in reducing the number of mouths to be fed and supplied with water, the latter more especially. Though this was a good beginning, I was by no means satisfied that all the dangerous element had been removed, and from time to time persistently urged my views to this effect, until eventually it seemed we had reduced the evil to a minimum. I cannot say that even yet (written August 14th) I am quite satisfied, but I hope and believe the internal danger is greatly reduced. Throughout we got no hearty assistance from the political officers, the *Wali*, or the city authorities, the chief of which (called the Kotwal) is, I believe, the prime villain of the lot, and I informed Colonel St. John (the political officer) that I considered he ought to be arrested, and that I should myself, on my own responsibility, assuredly seize him if there was the sign of an *emeute* in the town.

I have no doubt Colonel St. John will hereafter try to prove I was too decided, and too hard in this matter, but I am convinced I was right, and only wish I had more certainty that we were as safe from danger from within as he tries to make me believe. If I were General Primrose I would relieve him of all political powers while the present state of affairs lasted, and constitute myself only and chief political officer, and this I have urged on him. When I found it quite impossible, as it seemed to be at first, to move the Pathans out, I threatened (having received authority from General Primrose to act as might seem best) to throw a few shells into the Pathan quarter, and certainly would have done so when all other means failed, but never desired or wished to resort to so extreme a measure until all fair means had been tried.

July 31st.—After a quiet night I was up at 4.30 and sent out a reconnoitring party, which got well into cantonments without resistance, and returned almost unopposed. While, however, they were so employed, a large body of cavalry and infantry appeared on our right front, in the direction of Mandi Hissar, and occupied two villages within 1,000 yards of the wall. General Primrose ordered me to take out some cavalry and infantry to clear them off, which I did, and had a smart little fight, effecting our object, and killing about thirty of the enemy, with a loss to ourselves of one man killed and three wounded. I sent in to ask General Primrose to send me some guns, as the enemy had fallen back into a strong village, against the loopholed walls of which I did not care to rush the men until I had got a practicable breach.

No guns coming, and the object of the little expedition having been effected, I withdrew my party to the fort, where I found that General Primrose had not wished to push the affair further, and had sent to tell me so, but the message had not reached me. Hard at work all day improving our defences. Everyone is on duty always, and despite the hot sun and incessant labour, all are in first-rate health. Now the general regrets that he did not take advantage of the opportunity offered by the firing on our guards and picquets, to have all the cover, which lies round the city gates outside, down. It must all be done now, and as our working parties are always opposed, we lose men daily over the business. We all feel that we owe more than half our troubles and difficulties to the happy-go-lucky style adopted by General Stewart, who steadily objected to any military precautions whatever being taken at Kandahar. He is certainly the luckiest man in the world—having got safe away before his faults and oversights began to bear fruit.

August 1st.—Sent out very heavy working parties to clear the front of the Kabul Gate, which is a mass of houses and bazaars. These parties are relieved every four hours, and have to be protected by strong covering parties who are in conflict with the enemy the whole day, but both sides taking advantage of the cover afforded by the numerous walls, little serious loss results as a rule, though there is seldom a day that four, five, or more men are not killed and wounded. At 2 p.m. took direction of a small force to endeavour to find more of the Pathans, who are, I am confident, still lurking in the city intent on no good. It was a most unpleasant duty, but I hardened my heart, and made all I found go out. We got over 700 out on this occasion. I cannot say I am yet satisfied, and think we are being fooled and possibly betrayed by the *Wali* and his servants.

August 2nd.—Up at 5 a.m. to direct an attack on a garden opposite our S.W. bastion, which is the salient of my line of defence. Gave the executive charge to Colonel Bannerman, who carried out the affair in accordance with my instruction in an excellent manner, and most successfully, and though the resistance was steady, our loss was only one man killed and one wounded, the enemy losing very considerably.

August 3rd.—My birthday; forty-four years old today; could not help thinking much of all the dear ones at home, knowing how anxious they would be, and feeling sure I would not be forgotten on this day especially. Still working hard at our defences. The walls were divided into four sections for commands, as follows:—

General Primrose—The North or Eedgah Front.
General Burrows—W. or Herat Front.
General Nuttall—E. or Kabul Front.
General Brooke—S. or Shikarpore Front.

Though mine is shorter a good deal than either General Burrows' or General Nuttall, it has the drawback of being farthest from the citadel, and it is generally supposed it will be the one on which the heaviest attack will come. Each front is covered outside with a network of walls which must be destroyed.

August 4th.—All at the works. The enemy was rather troublesome, but a few shot and shell, and a steady fire from our selected marksmen, kept them off. The *Wali's* cavalry—about eighty men— went out of the Shikarpore Gate and looted some forage, about a mile to the front, in very good style. Prepared an abatis in front of my gate, and cut off the water supply of a village 1,000 yards due south. Slept on the ramparts, and visited all my line twice between 11 p.m. and 4 a.m. I have a camp bed up on the walls, but no one undresses, and sleep is taken in very small snatches. I may say now I live on my wall, as, except returning to the citadel for breakfast and dinner and a wash, I never leave the ramparts. We have rather a snug little mess, managed by Colonel Beville, consisting of General Burrows and his brigade major, Captain Law; Colonel Beville, and Captain Leckie, my brigade major, and myself. So far we have fared very comfortably, as there is a good deal to be bought, and we had a good deal of stores, &c., when we came in. I have quite given up any sort of wine or spirits during the day, and drink nothing but water or cold tea until dinner, when I have one glass of sherry, and sometimes a little hock and water, but generally, when I can get it, lime juice and water. I never touch spirits at all, and am convinced that for hard work there is nothing like drinks that do not inebriate.

August 5th.—Large covering and working parties in front of the Herat Gate to remove heavy cover between it and the general's old garden. Hardly any resistance offered by the enemy. I completed the abatis and wire entanglements opposite my gate, and the S.E. and S.W. bastions, both of which come within my charge. I consider the S.W. bastion the weakest point of my line, and the one where the heaviest and worst attack will be. I have a 40-pounder gun in the S.E. bastion, and two 9-pounders in the S.W. bastion. Urged thereto by General Burrows and myself, General Primrose had the Kotwal of the city arrested, and in the presence of General Burrows, Colonel St. John, the Nawab Hussun Ali, and myself, warned him of the precarious position in which he stood in case of any outbreak in the city, and told him of the reason of his arrest, &c. He was then conveyed to safe quarters, where he is kept under a European guard, no one seeing him except in the presence of the officer. I feel sure he was a traitor to us, and had some bad scheme in contemplation, and his arrest will nip his machinations in the bud. Even Colonel St. John was glad he was arrested.

August 6th.—At 3 a.m. every man was turned out and occupied the post he would hold in case of attack, to ascertain that all knew their places. Everything was very quietly done, and the arrangements worked well. The working parties in front of my gate were much annoyed by the enemy firing at long distances. One officer, Lieutenant De Trafford, 7th Fusiliers, was wounded. We brought down a mortar and cleared out one of the most troublesome villages, Ayoob Khan's camp was observed to be pitched behind Picquet Hill in the old cantonments.

August 7th.—Threw some shells (40-pounders) with excellent effect into Ayoob's camp. A regular stampede ensued, and many tents were seen to be on fire, and the camp was quickly deserted. The distance from us being 3,500 yards (two miles) they thought they were quite safe, and their horror and astonishment was all the greater. We heard afterwards that one shell had killed ten and wounded two men, burning down the tent in which they were lying. Busy all day on my walls improving the fire capacity which, owing to the peculiar formation of the walls and towers, is very defective, and, do what we may, will never be really good. The heat is very great, inducing great lassitude, which is not wonderful, seeing one barely gets four hours sleep out of twenty-four, and never has one's clothes off except for one's tub, the great luxury of the day, and which I always have now just before dinner.

August 8th.—Heavy firing from the enemy on the working parties in front of the Dourani and Kabul Gates, and it took a serious administration of mortar shells to quiet the enemy. For the first time the enemy opened their artillery on us from a well constructed battery on Picquet Hill. Our 40-pounder at the N.W. angle, however, made excellent practice, and dismounted one of their guns. The enemy have moved their camp to a position beyond Abasabad, 5,000 yards from our guns. They are busy throwing up batteries against the Herat face.

August 9th.—Large working and covering parties (under Colonel Daubeny) in front of the S.W. bastion to complete necessary demolitions. We lost several men, killed and wounded, but did good work. A large force of the enemy collected in the village opposite Shikarpore Gate, but were turned out by our mortar fire. It was proposed to attack the village of Deh Kojah, which is 900 yards from the Kabul Gate, in view to inflicting a lesson on the enemy. It was clear we could not think of holding it, or any other place beyond the walls, and therefore we should have no real advantage to recompense us for the certain loss the enterprise would entail. For many good reasons I objected to the plan, as useless and involving a certain heavy loss and discouragement to the men, and eventually it was given up, a short bombardment being substituted for it, which was, I fear, not very useful either.

August 10th.—Quiet night; but at 6.30 a.m. enemy opened, on the S.W. bastion, with a gun which had been placed in position during the night in village opposite Shikarpore Gate. The shells fell short, doing no damage, and our artillery forced him to evacuate the position. Enemy appear to be busy throwing up entrenchments on Picquet Hill, also in a corner of the garden opposite S.W. bastion. He threw some shells into the citadel, one bursting in a room next to the church. For the first time I had leisure, and went round and visited all the wounded officers and men, all doing well, though Major Iredell's wound is very serious. Threw some shells into enemy's work in front of S.W. bastion. Effect not satisfactory, and the distance being only 400 yards, portions of the shells flew back over us, and one bit killed one of our mules.

On going my rounds at 10 p.m. I heard decided indications of men at work in the village opposite the Shikarpore Gate, and also sounds of wheels (artillery), from which I judged the enemy were throwing up a battery there. Reinforced parties on walls, and remained expecting an attack all night, but none came.

August 11th.—At daylight discovered that the village in front of my gate has, as I anticipated, been much fortified since the previous evening, but were quite unable to discover where the battery, if there is one, is placed. Letters received for the first time from India, but only two in cipher, for General Primrose and Colonel St. John. By them we are informed that Sir F. Roberts left Kabul on the 7th, with a division to assist us—he cannot be here before the 1st of next month—and that General Phayre was doing all he could to gather a force to bring to our relief. He was at Quetta on the 6th, so it is unlikely that he either can arrive until the end of the month. Bombarded village in front of Shikarpore Gate with good effect.

August 12th.—A quiet night. Being grouse-shooting day, we acted as grouse, and were heavily shot at as we had a large covering and working party out opposite the S.W. bastion, in hopes of effecting some much wanted demolitions. The whole were under the command of Lieutenant-Colonel Griffiths, 1st Native Infantry, who, in my judgement, by no means made the most of his opportunities, and little or no work was done. The gardens which had to be taken were full of the enemy, who were, however, smartly driven out by the Fusiliers and 19th Native Infantry, but owing to supports not being brought up, the enemy returned in force, and the position became untenable, unless we wished to precipitate a general action, which was undesirable.

All sorts of wild reports were sent in of large gatherings of the enemy approaching, which I did not credit, but it was considered wiser to recall the parties, which was done, and all fell back under a fierce fire, during which many of our men fell. I was standing on the parapet, directing matters as far as I could, when I witnessed, just twenty feet beneath me, a grand piece of gallantry on the part of two young Royal Engineer officers (Lieutenants Jones and Waller), who, under a galling fire, returned from safe cover and carried into safety a wounded sepoy, during which operation one of the men who was with them, a private of the 7th, was killed—shot through the head. I can personally testify to the hotness of the fire, and I have recommended both for the Victoria Cross, which I think they fully deserve. I am opposed altogether to these small fights which cost many lives and have but little results, but the next there is I shall, I think, take myself and try to make a better job of it than was done today.

August 13th.—Quiet night and morning. Not a soul to be

seen all round. After breakfast went on the signal tower to watch the effect of a few 40-pounder shells, which we were going to throw into the enemy's new camp, at 5,000 yards' range. The shots were excellent, and evidently created much consternation, but the enemy had evidently seen our group on the signal tower, and at once sent a 12-pounder shell at us, which went beyond the tower, his second trial was short and went into the city, but his third shot was so far successful that he hit the lower part of the tower. At 6 p.m. we shelled a battery in Deh Khoja. The enemy replied briskly for half an hour, and then finding it too hot, shut up. On this occasion we used 7-pounder shells in the 9-pounder guns, to which they had been adapted by an ingenious contrivance of Major Caldecott. They proved a great success, and are a grand addition to our firing powers, as we have 1,100 of them in the arsenal.

On coming back to the walls after dinner I found a telegram from the Herat Gate, to say that large bodies of men were advancing with music, &c. Knowing the anxious nature of my friend in command there the information did not much excite me, and I waited till I could get down to the S.W. bastion before deciding if any special measures were necessary. Getting there I heard the music (most discordant), and concluded it was in the engineer garden in our old cantonments, and was merely the enemy having a musical evening. The fact that there was music was rather a proof that the enemy did not contemplate an attack. There were, no doubt, many people about, but on the whole I decided there was nothing at the moment worth turning out the garrison for, so sent a re-assuring telegram to headquarters, which was justified by a quiet night.

August 14th.—At 6.30 the enemy opened a battery on the Shikarpore Gate, to which we quickly replied, shutting him and his guns up in half an hour. A spy came in who reports our shells have created much damage among the enemy; also that they lost sixty men in the little affair of the 12th, among them Mahomed Azim Khan, Governor of Furrah, a very great man indeed. The spy says there is an artillery officer prisoner with Ayoub Khan, and that he is very well treated in every way; he also says that the enemy have 1,500 wounded now lying at Maiwand.

Here the *Diary* ends!

Appendix

Sergeant-Major T. Rickard, of the 2/7th Fusiliers, states:—

On the 16th August, 1880, I was one of the party ordered out for the storming of Deh Khoja, under General Brooke. We attacked the village at the south end about 5.30 a.m. under a very heavy fire in all directions from the enemy. When we arrived in the centre of the village, Captain Cruikshank, R.E., got wounded. General Brooke assisted in helping him along. We then advanced further on, to force our way through the village, when we halted and got under a wall, as we thought under cover, but the enemy's fire from all directions kept getting heavier, and the longer we stopped the heavier the fire got. General Brooke said to me, "Sergeant-Major, we shall never get out of this, I am afraid." He then ordered us to retire back out of the village. We did so. After we got out of the village about 300 yards, we halted again under cover about ten minutes, and fired on the enemy as fast as we could. General Brooke asked me to send him another man to help him along with Captain Cruikshank.

I did so, and we retired again towards the fort, and had only got about 200 yards when General Brooke was shot in the head (dead), and the other man that was helping was shot. I was with General Brooke the whole time, till he was shot.

T. Rickard,

Sergeant-Major 2/7th Royal Fusiliers.

From Col. French, R.A., Comm. Artillery in Kandahar.

Kandahar, 26th August.

My Dear Annie,

Most sincerely do I sympathize with you in the loss of your dear good husband, poor Henry; he was so genial, cheery, kind, and courteous to all who came in contact with him, and much beloved and respected by everyone in this force. No braver or truer soldier lost his life in that ill-fated attack on Deh Khoja. I miss him so very much, we were thrown so much together during the last four months. No man was more keen for a fight than poor Henry, and when the day of battle did come, right gallantly he led his men, sacrificing his life in the humane effort to rescue a wounded man from falling into the hands of the enemy. From Trumpeter McGlynn, C/2 R.A., who was his orderly trumpeter on the 16th August, I have heard the following account of how poor Henry fell:—

After half an hour's skirmishing they reached the village, and on entering, Henry and the Trumpeter had just dismounted, when a volley from the enemy so startled their horses they broke away, and galloped back to within the city. Henry advanced through the village on foot, cheering on his men amidst a galling fire of musketry, which the enemy poured on them from loop-holed walls. Arrived in the centre of the village, Captain Cruikshank, R.E., fell badly wounded.

At this time our men were being driven back by superior numbers and the heavy fire from the houses. Henry helped to carry Cruikshank; succeeded in getting him out of the village, of which they had got clear about thirty yards, Henry still supporting Cruikshank, when he was struck down by apparently a bullet in the head. Trumpeter McGlynn states that he fell forward on his face and never moved after; so poor Henry's death must have been instantaneous.

The trumpeter and a few men of the 7th Fusiliers tried to carry off the body, but were compelled to desist owing to the enemy making a rush on them. Deh Khoja was evacuated on the night of the 24th, and on the following day search was made for the bodies of our fallen. Henry's was found and buried near where he fell, under a Peepul tree, the Rev. Mr. Cane, our chaplain, having read the burial service. This terrible loss of life at Maiwand and Deh Khoja has cast a gloom on all here, and no man is more generally sorrowed for and regretted than poor Henry—every inch a soldier. No man worked harder to put this city in a state of defence. I looked upon him as one of our rising generals, who, later on, would have shone out with much distinction.

From Colonel B————.
Kandahar, 14th September, 1880.
My dear Major H.,

I am sorry I have been unable, through press of work, to fulfil my promise before now, and send you the particulars of the unfortunate affair of Deh Khoja, on the 16th August, as far as they are known by me, which cost us so many valuable lives, and more especially that of my dear friend General Brooke; whose loss was deeply felt by everyone here, for he was not only much loved by all, but he had proved himself to be possessed of the greatest energy and cool good judgement, and had consequently gained the confidence of all ranks, both senior and junior. I have no hesitation in saying that we are indebted to him for much that was done to strengthen our position here, and in the arrangements for the defence.

He never rested until he got the Pathans turned out of the city, and the place disarmed. How much he did do, and how much his wise influence effected will probably never be known fully by the public; but from a perusal of his *Diary* which I gave you, it will be seen how continually active he was in carrying out the work assigned to him, and what his opinions were on many subjects. He was strongly opposed to the attack on Deh Khoja, for many reasons, which he gives in his *Diary*, and he was mainly instrumental in its being abandoned the week before, when it had been resolved on.

The attack was finally decided on, the following week, on the advice, I believe, of the commanding engineer, in consequence of our working parties employed outside the Kabul Gate, in demolishing some buildings, having been prevented by the fire from Deh Khoja completing the work. His objections to it were stronger than before, as it was known that the enemy had been busily employed all the week in fortifying the village, and he feared that the loss would be greater than we could afford, or than the good to be gained. He could not, however, urge his objections, as he had done on the previous occasion, as he was nominated to command the attack. The force was composed of 300 cavalry, 300 royal fusiliers, and 500 native infantry.

The cavalry left the Eedgar Gate at 4 o'clock in the morning, and making a wide detour of the village of Kairabad took up a position in the rear of Deh Khoja, *i.e.,* on the west. Our guns on the walls then commenced a bombardment to prepare the Infantry attack, and at 5.0 a.m. the infantry moved out of the Kabul Gate, covered by riflemen from the walls.

Immediately they got out into the open they came under a very heavy fire from the village, which is from 700 to 800 yards from the city, but the troops advanced in splendid form and were never once checked. They entered the village at the south, as had been previously decided on, and we then lost sight of them, but we could hear them hard at work with their rifles. I need not describe the village, for you have seen it and know what a labyrinth of narrow streets and high walls it is, every enclosure being a regular little fortification, so that as soon as the enemy was driven out of one position they ran into another like a lot of rats, and our force was too weak to hold the positions as they were taken.

General Brooke, however, pushed on with his troops right through the village from south to north, and leaving a strong party of the fusiliers at the latter part, he retraced his steps with a view of completing the capture, but by this time the enemy began to pour in from the south of the village; these were reinforcements sent by Ayoob Khan from the cantonments as soon as he had heard the firing going on. They advanced by the gardens and village on the south of the city, which afforded them shelter from our fire until they came opposite our S. E. bastion where we had a 40-pounder and 9-pounder which gave them several rounds, but did not do them much damage, the practice being bad. It did not at any rate check them.

Our cavalry, however, seeing them coming, moved down in that direction and stopped them for some little time, but being exposed to a heavy fire from the enclosures when they could not act, they had to be withdrawn. On finding that the enemy were crowding into the village from the south, General Brooke sent his brigade-major to General Primrose to report matters and to ask for orders, the reply to which was to retire his Force at once, but by the time this officer got back to the village the enemy held it in such force he could not get to General Brooke, who was still in the centre of it.

A trumpeter of C/2, who was with General Brooke all the time, informed me that when they returned from the north of the village and had reached about the centre, they found Captain Cruikshank, R.E., severely wounded, and unable to move, and finding that the enemy was closing in on them all round, General Brooke looked out for some defensible place into which he could get the party which was with him, consisting of men of the fusiliers and native sappers, and for this purpose he made for a courtyard in which there were buildings, but directly they entered it they were met by a heavy fire.

It was here that Captain Cruikshank begged him to leave him to his fate, and save himself and party, but he nobly refused to do this, and thinking there were still some of his party in the south of the village where he had left them, he determined to push on in that direction, so calling for volunteers of the fusiliers to carry poor Cruikshank, they moved down to the south under a heavy fire and got out into the open. All the parties had been compelled to withdraw, and there was nothing left for them but to make the best of their way back to the city, taking advantage of what cover they could find. They were much hampered by having to carry poor Cruikshank, and they had frequently to change the men who were carrying him.

It was during one of these changes, when they had got about

100 yards from the village, and poor Brooke was supporting Cruikshank with his left arm while the men were being relieved, that he was shot through the back, just between the shoulders, and fell dead; at the same time a number of *Ghazis* made a rush on them from the village, and the remainder of the party retreated hastily towards the city. On the 25th August the village was evacuated by the enemy, and we went out to bury the bodies. I found and recognised poor Brooke's body. He was lying among several others, and Cruikshank and a Sergeant Strong were close to him. It was a fearfully melancholy sight, but it was a great satisfaction to recover the bodies and to give them burial, which we did under a tree close to the spot where they fell.

While deeply grieving and lamenting over his death and those who died with him, one cannot but feel proud of his noble and gallant conduct in sacrificing himself in endeavouring to save a brother officer. Among the papers which I gave you, you will find one containing his views on the situation in Afghanistan, which will repay perusal, and which will, no doubt, be valuable to his family. I have his sword, which I forgot to give you with the other things I had selected to send home. I will take care of it till I get an opportunity of sending it home.

From Mrs. L———.
11th October.
My dear B———,
I am enclosing one sheet of the letter which was written on the 16th August, the day of the sortie.

"Kandahar, August 16th.
"This is a very sad day for us. There was a great sortie this morning against a village outside the Kabul Gate. We sent out 800 infantry and 300 cavalry under General Brooke. They got into the village, and there they suffered considerable loss. The fusiliers lost two officers, Marsh and Wood, both young boys, twenty-five killed, and twenty-nine wounded; the 28th one officer, Colonel Newport, killed, and thirty killed and nineteen wounded; the 19th two officers, Major Trench and Lieutenant Stayner, killed.

Their return of men have not yet come in. Major Vandeleur, 7th Fusiliers, is badly wounded; Colonel Nimmo, 28th, dangerously; Colonel Shewell, of the commissariat, wounded; Lieutenant Wood, of the transport, badly wounded; Captain Cruikshank, of the engineers, killed; the Rev. Gordon, dangerously wounded; and last and worst, General Brooke killed.

"I feel so sad about it, I can hardly speak, for I had learnt almost to love him, indeed I may say quite. He was shot through the head as he was carrying poor Cruikshank away from the village; and the worst of it is, that, in the opinion of many of us, this sortie was a quite useless waste of life.

I believe we inflicted considerable loss of life on the enemy; but it was mere madness attacking with such a small force, a labyrinth of lanes and houses like that. Brooke knew it, but could not protest, as he was ordered to command the force. Burrows knew it, but he was not consulted. A man of the fusiliers, whom I questioned about Brooke's death, says, the party he was with would never have got out of the village but for him. He is a great loss, for he was the best head we had, and I think the whole Force deplores his loss, nearly—though not quite as much as I do.

"When you write to B——, let her and her husband know how he was loved, and how nobly he died. I cannot write any more. There is a great deal to be done; but no more sorties, I trust. We ought merely to have waited, but somebody got an idea we ought to do something."

Poor Brooke was warned that he was going to certain death when he went back for Cruikshank, but he would go. Cruikshank was mortally wounded, and begged them to leave him and save themselves. Brooke had ordered the cavalry to cover the retreat of the Infantry, which was construed into an order to retire, and the consequence was that the cavalry was withdrawn, and crowds of men rushed into the village, which had been kept in check on the far side of the cavalry—even before our men were out of the village. I cannot tell you how I miss Brooke, he was always so cheery and jolly, and had such sound views; he was the best head we had in the force.

In another letter he says, "Brooke's loss shows day by day more seriously; his cheery temper and sound views had the best influence.

"We miss his counsels greatly, in another way he is a great loss, as he knew every yard of the country round, and would have been the very man to lead a turning column. If it were not for the loss of Brooke, I should feel quite jolly, but I can't get him out of my head."

From Mrs. P———
21st October, 1880.
Dear Mr. Brooke,
We had this morning letters from my brother Colonel H., at Kandahar, and we think you would like to hear what he says of your brother. To my husband my brother writes:—Poor Brooke, as gallant a fellow as ever stepped, led the attack, and after doing gallant deeds was recalled by the orders of General Primrose (from the walls of the city), and in retiring and trying to save a brother officer's life lost his own. The three columns, as is invariably the case, lost all sight and touch of each other, and nobody knew, where .the others were; in spite of it all, the effect on the enemy was very great, and the siege to all intents and purposes ended.

Poor Brooke was full of zeal and energy, and died a soldier's death in being the last to leave the village, and in attempting to carry poor Cruikshank, who had been fatally wounded, out of action. It may be a satisfaction to Mrs. Brooke to know that he behaved so gallantly and was spared all suffering while carrying his brother officer under a most murderous fire.

Twenty-four were killed round about him, and the heaviest loss occurred where he fell; he did not retire of his own accord, and was greatly surprised to get the order which was sent him by General Primrose; on receiving it he sent orders for the several parties to retire, and fell back himself last of all with a few men. Being ordered to retire, he had no opportunity to carry out his plan to the end; it might have been a grand success or a heavy loss, but his loss was very heavily felt by the force.

In the Battle of Pir Paimal we formed, with one of Roberts' brigades, the reserve, while two brigades attacked. Our reserve had a grand chance of distinguishing themselves, and had Brooke been alive, I believe it would have been done.

From Colonel ———.

Kandahar, September, 1880.

Brooke was constantly at General Primrose about our weakness in Troops and the defencelessness of the citadel, but he would never sanction any money being spent on it. Everything he did, or rather did not do, was bad enough, but I shall never forgive him the Deh Khoja business on the 16th August, which lost us poor Brooke's life, and the lives of so many brave men, without any object.

General Primrose had ordered the assault on Deh Khoja the week before, but Brooke and Burrows got him to countermand it for the following reasons, namely:—The village was built of thick mud walls and roofs, so that it could not possibly be burned; it was known to be very strongly held by the enemy, and would therefore require a large force to take it, and we should therefore lose a great many more men than we could spare, and if we captured it we could not hold it, as we had not enough men to man our own walls properly, and as it could not be burned, or destroyed, or held, the enemy would simply walk back into it the minute we left it; and the last and best reason was, that as there were two forces coming to our relief, our duty was to hold Kandahar, and do nothing to endanger our position, and certainly not to go outside the walls to fight the enemy, giving up the advantage that we had.

We all thought the insane idea had been given up for good, but the following week General Primrose sent for Brooke and Burrows, and told them that he had made up his mind to attack the village next morning, and told Brooke he was to command the force.

This, of course, effectually prevented Brooke saying what he thought, as he told me he could not raise objections against it, under these circumstances, as it might be thought that he was afraid, but he said, "the objections against it are greater than they were before, as it is known that the enemy have been hard at work all the week fortifying the place." Burrows ought to have done his best to oppose it, but as Brooke did not oppose, for the above reason he, said nothing, and so the attack unfortunately took place the next morning. Being on the headquarter staff, I was not, of course, allowed to go, but I watched it from the walls where our riflemen covered the advance of the attacking party and our big guns.

The village of Deh Khoja was only 700 yards off, and the enemy fired at us tremendously. The troops advanced under a very heavy fire, very steadily and well, and entered the village and went right through it, but the place was like a rabbit warren right through it, with very large loop-holed walls, from which the enemy kept up an incessant fire without our men being able to see them, and as soon as they were turned out of one enclosure they ran into another, and back again into those they had been turned out of, for our forces were not strong enough to hold the enclosures as they were taken, and all this time the enemy was pouring into the village from Ayoub Khan's main force.

At last General Primrose sent to order the force to retreat, and no doubt poor Brooke could have got away unhurt, but he stopped to bring away a wounded officer, and so lost his life. We did not recover the bodies of the killed until the 25th, ten days after, when the village was deserted by the enemy. I went to search for poor Brooke, whom I recognised, and I buried him myself. I cannot get over his loss.

We have lived together since we came here, and I have become very fond of him; I am sure he liked me, and that I have lost a good friend in him. He was a fine fellow, brave as a lion, and a thorough soldier in every way; clear-headed and with excellent judgement. It is indeed grievously sad such a fine fellow should have been lost, for he is a loss to the whole army, in such a needless manner.

From Lieutenant F———.
26th February, 1881.
My dear Mrs. Brooke,

He (General Brooke) was quite against the sortie, but being put in command of it he was obliged to keep quiet. General Nuttall, who commanded the cavalry, and who was senior to General Brooke, was ordered to co-operate with him. After our infantry, with whom General Brooke was, had penetrated into the village, the general found that he could not hold it, and sent a note in pencil to General Nuttall, who was with the cavalry, which was drawn up in line to the south of Deh Khoja, and thus between it and the villages to the south, asking him to cover the retreat from Deh Khoja. However, General Primrose, who was looking on from the walls just about this time, sent his orderlies, one to General Brooke, the other to General Nuttall, ordering them both to retire.

General Nuttall received the order immediately after getting General Brooke's note, and instead of doing what the latter requested, retired his cavalry at once to the city. The result was that the villagers of all the southern villages instantly swarmed round Deh Khoja, and cut off the retreat of the infantry. These poor fellows had to run for their lives through a gauntlet of fire. General Brooke got safely out of the village, but went back with a few men to aid others, and in trying to save Captain Cruikshank, of the Engineers, was shot through the head and killed instantly. This, I believe, is the full account of the disaster, which would not have occurred, if the cavalry had remained to cover the retreat.

From Colonel B———.
Kandahar, *5th December*, 1880.
My dear Mrs. Brooke,

We had lived together up here, and I had learnt to love him as a brother, for he was all that was noble and kind and generous, and I felt his sad loss most truly and most deeply. I shall never forget that fearful morning as long as I live. I was distracted when the remnants of the force returned and he was not with it. I fear I forgot everyone else in my grief at losing my dearest friend, and the one head in whom we all placed full reliance and faith, and regarding whom we universally felt, as long as he was with us, all would be well. I can assure you, dear Mrs. Brooke, he was beloved by everyone here, and his loss was universally mourned for as the greatest one that could have happened to us, for every one appreciated his splendid soldier-like qualities and clear-headed abilities, and as to his courage and determination it was the admiration of everyone, so you must not think he was not loved and valued here, for I have no hesitation in saying that he possessed the love and confidence of everybody, for everybody went to him for advice, and he never refused it to anyone.

Would that General Primrose had taken his advice, and stuck to it alone, and then that wretched sortie would never have taken place. I handed over his Letts' rough diary to Major H., and in that he records his opinion on the sortie when ordered the week before, and which he prevented. Unfortunately, as he told me himself, his mouth was closed on the second occasion, as he was ordered to command the attacking force, and it would appear. as if he was afraid, and besides he had given General Primrose his opinion very clearly about it, on the previous occasion, and. the objections and arguments, he then made against it, had become stronger, for it was known that the enemy had been busily engaged all the week fortifying the place.

I will not relate again the particulars of that sad day, as I feel sure you must have, before now, received the long account I sent through Major H., and it is very painful to me to refer to it; suffice it to say, that your dear Husband fell as a true and brave soldier, nobly endeavouring to save the life of poor Captain Cruikshank, after having remained to the very last in the village to collect all the remaining men and bring them out. He might, no doubt, have secured his own safety by retiring himself sooner, but he was not the man to do so, as long as he thought there was anyone else left behind, and in fact he was coming out with Colonel Daubeny's party of the fusiliers, by the north of the village, when he returned; to satisfy himself that no one was left behind, and he went right through the place again, and came out by the south, and it was then, I understand, he found Captain Cruikshank and endeavoured to bring him out. I am sure it will be a consolation to you to know that he fell perfectly dead, and never suffered any pain. I had this direct from his Trumpeter orderly, a European, who was with him all the time, and by his side when he fell. I examined him most minutely on this point, and he assured me he never spoke a word when he fell, and I found a wound through his body caused by a bullet, which must have caused instant death.

From Col. C———.

Kandahar, 11th January, 1881.

My dear Annie,

Very few enjoy such general respect and admiration when living, or when gone cause such universal expressions of praise and regret. I am now living with the 7th Fusiliers, and I assure you when I came up, and now when alluded to, no officer seemed then, or now, to be able to say enough in praise of his late brigadier, and many have some kind act or word to record, as either received at his hands or spoken to them during the siege.

In the *Bombay Gazette* of the 1st inst., there is an article in which the way in which brigade commands are given, often to people who have never, since boy service, done anything but staff work in an office, is spoken of, and asking how such officers, save in certain exceptions, can be expected to be efficient in the field, and it goes on to say,

"we have on more than one occasion testified to our admiration of General Brooke's splendid qualities as a soldier, while, as time goes on, the heroic manner of his death will more and more command admiration."

I don't think in March, when the appointment was made, there was a dissenting voice or a doubt expressed that it was otherwise than the best that could be made. On the last night of the old year there was a large fire in the citadel square, round which all the soldiers had been singing; on our going out after mess to join them, they sang a song all about the siege and sortie, recounting where and how they had lost their Brigadier, officers, and men, the chorus of which was—

"All honour now to General Brooke,
Who in his grave does lie,
And fighting for Queen and country,
Did like a soldier die."

Of course it is soldier's language, but it nevertheless is expressive of their feelings.

From Captain C———.

General Brooke was respected and beloved by every man and officer in the Force, and esteemed by everyone. He gave me my orders on that fatal day, when he fell, and I was never near him afterwards, for he met his death, with one of our colour-sergeants, while nobly assisting Captain Cruikshank, R.E., who was badly wounded; but the name of General Brooke will long be remembered, and in his death we have lost one of our best officers.

The English army met with a great loss in General Brooke, beloved and respected as he was by all the brigade.

General Brooke was beloved by all who knew him, and the soldiers worshipped him.

EXTRACT FROM THE *IRISH TIMES*, AUGUST 25TH, 1880.

Afghanistan.

The Sortie From Kandahar.

Heavy British Losses.

List of Killed and Wounded Officers.

"From Viceroy, August 24.

"Following from St. John, Kandahar, 21st:—Sortie took place on 16th against village on east face of city. Has secured us from further molestation on that side, but loss very heavy.

"Killed.

"Brigadier-General Brooke, Captain Cruikshank, R.E.; Colonel Newport, 28th; Major Trench, Lieutenant Stayner, 19th; Lieutenants Marsh and Wood, Fusiliers, and Rev. Mr. Gordon.

"Wounded.

"Colonel Nimmo, 28th; Major Vandeleur, 7th; and Lieutenant Wood, Transport (all severely); Colonels Malcolmson and Shewell

"Casualties among men, about 180.

"A messenger has also come in from Kandahar. The position there is regarded as perfectly safe. A sortie was made on the 16th, and Colonel St. John reports that its result has been to secure the east face of the city from further molestation.

"The enemy must, however, have fought with great determination, as our loss is heavy, especially in officers.

"We have lost in killed and wounded, about 180 men. Of officers, General Brooke, Colonel Newport, of the 28th Regiment; Major Trench, and Lieutenant Stayner, of the 19th Regiment; Captain Cruikshank, R. E.; Lieutenants Marsh and Wood, of the 7th Fusiliers; and the Rev. Mr. Gordon, are killed. Colonel Nimmo, of the 28th; Major Vandeleur, of the 7th, and Lieutenant Wood, of the Transport Corps, severely wounded; and Colonels Malcolmson and Shewell, slightly wounded.

"General Brooke was killed while carrying Cruikshank, wounded, out of action."

28th August.
181
General Order
By
His Excellency the Commander-in-Chief.

Adjutant-General's Office, Head Quarters, Poona,
28th August, 1880.

It is with much regret that the commander-in-chief has to announce the death of Brigadier-General H. F. Brooke, adjutant-general, Bombay army.

Brigadier-General Brooke having been selected for the command of a brigade in Southern Afghanistan was, at the time of his death, engaged in command of a sortie made by the Garrison of Kandahar, and is reported to have been killed whilst endeavouring to succour a wounded brother officer.

His Excellency desires to place on record his appreciation of the valuable services and willing assistance rendered at all times by the late Brigadier-General Brooke, and the high estimation in which his abilities and soldierly qualities were held by all who knew him.

The commander-in-chief feels sure that all ranks will sympathise with him in the loss the service has sustained in the noble death of so able an officer, whilst gallantly engaged in the performance of his duties on active service in the field.

By order of His Excellency the Commander-in-Chief,
Alex. Wardrop, Lieutenant-Colonel,
Officiating Adjutant-General.

Death of Brigadier-General Brooke.

We regret to announce the death of this gallant gentleman, which took place under circumstances rendering the event very sad indeed. Brigadier-General Henry Francis Brooke, who was only forty-four years of age, was in command of the 2nd Infantry Brigade Kandahar Field Force, and took part in the sortie from the garrison on the 16th of August, which resulted in securing the east face of the city from further molestation by the besieging force. He had come out of action unhurt; but with a humanity which adds lustre to his gallantry, he endeavoured to carry away a wounded brother officer, Captain Cruikshank, R.E., and while engaged in this act of friendship and of mercy he was killed by a shot from the enemy.

Brigadier-General Brooke was eldest son of the late Mr. G. Brooke and Lady Arabella Brooke, of Ashbrooke, in the County Fermanagh, and was of the same family as Sir Victor Brooke, Bart., of Colebrooke, in that County. He entered the army in June, 1854, and his promotion was as follows:—Lieutenant, May, '55; Captain, September, '58; Major, February, '61; Lieutenant-Colonel December, '71; Colonel, February, '77. In April, 1855, he landed in the Crimea with the 48th Regiment, and served at the siege and fall of Sebastopol, for which he obtained a medal with clasp and a Turkish medal. He served also throughout the campaign of 1860 in China, as *aide-de-camp* to Sir Robert Napier, and was present at the actions of Sinho and Tangku, the assault of the Taku Forts, at which he was severely wounded, and the final advance on and surrender of Pekin, for which he received a medal with two clasps and the brevet-rank of major. Subsequently he held the post of adjutant-general in Bombay, with the local rank of brigadier-general. He was a gallant officer, sprung from a gallant race, and one more of those brave men who have sustained and increased the military fame of Fermanagh.

Brigadier-General Brooke.

Brigadier-General Henry Francis Brooke, killed in the sortie at Kandahar on the 16th August, is the first general officer of Her Majesty's army who has fallen in action since 1858. The last two instances were those of brigadier-generals the Hon. Adrian Hope and Penny, C.B., who were killed within three weeks of each other, the former officer in Oude and the latter in Rohilcund. The sad circumstances of the gallant Adrian Hope's death will long be remembered, as well as the causes which led to the sacrifice of so many precious lives through the rashness of General Walpole.

The late Brigadier-General Brooke was one of the youngest colonels in our army, he having obtained his brevet-colonelcy in less than twenty-three years after his entry into the service. He joined the army in June, 1854, and as a subaltern landed with the 48th Foot in the Crimea on the 21st April, 1855, serving at the siege and fall of Sebastopol. After the war he accompanied the 48th to India, and went as *aide-de-camp* to Sir Robert Napier on the China expedition, serving throughout the campaign of 1860, and taking part in the actions of Sinho and Tangku, the assault of the Taku Forts (severely wounded), and the final advance on and surrender of Pekin.

For his China services he received a brevet majority, dated the 15th February, 1861. He afterwards exchanged into the 94th, and was selected for staff employ in the Bengal Presidency at the close of 1864, when he was appointed assistant adjutant-general of the Presidency Division. Colonel Brooke was subsequently assistant adjutant-general at Mean Meer, and in November, 1877, was selected to succeed Brigadier Aitchison as adjutant-general of the Bombay army. On the formation of a Bombay corps for service in Afghanistan, Brigadier Brooke was one of the first officers selected for command, and was sent to Kandahar with

General Primrose. He bore a very high reputation in the service as a first-rate officer, and his loss will be greatly felt, especially at such a crisis when reliable leaders are so much needed at the seat of war.

The deceased belonged to an old Irish family, the Brookes, of Colebrooke, County Fermanagh, and was a cousin of the Earl of Huntington, his mother, Lady Arabella Hastings, having been a sister of the late peer. An uncle of the deceased, Lieutenant Francis Brooke, 7th Dragoon Guards, was slain at Waterloo. The family has furnished our army with several officers of distinction.

It seems to us that the death of Colonel Brooke in the sortie of the 16th was a peculiarly sad one. No doubt it was the death which this gallant and distinguished officer would have preferred. It was, we take it, a soldier's death, realised at the head of his men. But there are enemies and enemies, and certainly a soldier might be excused if he shrank from having his throat cut by a fanatic, fighting in a cause which on the British side is not by any means clear. Colonel Brooke, as our notice of his service will show, had led a brilliant military career. He entered the army in time to take part in the Crimea war, and was present at the siege and fall of Sebastopol. Subsequently he shared the perils of the war in China, and was engaged in the assault on the Taku Forts, where he was severely wounded. It is true that a British officer must be prepared to face death wherever he may be sent to meet his country's enemies.

But in the Crimea and in China there was a tangible object to be realised sufficient to justify the campaign, and to lift the enterprise from the miserable conflict which is now being raged, through no fault of ours, in Afghanistan. Colonel Brooke, like other gallant officers and men who have fallen with him, adds very heavily to the already too heavy losses of the war in Afghanistan.—*Broad Arrow.*

The Late Captain Cruikshank, R.E.

To the Editor of the *Bombay Gazette*.

Sir,—I venture to send you the accompanying extract from a letter received from Kandahar, thinking that the many friends of the late Captain Cruikshank, R.E., may like to know how highly he was thought of. If a dark cloud at present hangs over the Bombay army, here at least is the "silver lining" amid the general gloom. Poor Cruikshank was a great friend of mine, as indeed, he would be of anyone who got to know him well. His duty was to blow up the walls of Deh Khoja with gunpowder. He dined with me on the 15th, and was as cool in talking over his work for next morning as if it were the ordinary work. He went out to the village, and set about his mining operations in the same cool way. When he received his first wound, either in the side or in the hip, General Brooke helped him outside the city (village) walls, and then got him into a *doolie*, but, I suppose, the *doolie*-bearers fled. Then General Brooke would not leave him, and they died side by side.

All the wounds received that day were very severe ones, as all were in such close quarters, and the enemy, posted on roofs, shot downwards. Cruikshank was thus shot. The enemy rushed out on our retreating troops, and cut them up at once, so poor Cruikshank would not be long left in pain. When I saw his body, ten days after, it was clear his end had been speedy. The body was not, however, mutilated at all. His clothes were left on, and his butler's watch, with some maps, were found in his pocket. He was a very regular communicant, and even during the siege, when he was worked on Sunday as hard as on other days, he generally (if not always) managed to get to church for the midday service.

He communicated last on the 15th of August, *i.e.,* the day before he died. I had formed a very high opinion of poor Cruikshank as an R. E. officer. He always seemed to me to be at work, and never seemed to talk about it; so after his death I asked his commanding officer if I had formed a too high opinion of him, and I should wish any of poor Cruikshank's friends to have heard his reply. He said he would sooner have lost any two men in the garrison, not excluding the highest, than poor Cruikshank. He always did any work he was put to, at once, and well. For days and days he worked away outside under the walls, exposed to the enemy's fire, and never seemed to think of it. His commanding officer said he deserved a V.C., and had he lived he would have tried to get it for him. I can't tell you half he (the C.O.) said, but I never heard an officer so spoken of by his immediate superiors in my life before. Alas, that sad day, the 16th of August, which saw such noble spirits, Brooke and Cruikshank, who were indeed "lovely and pleasant in their lives, and in death were not divided," left dead upon that fatal field.—I am, &c,

His most intimate friend.

ALSO FROM LEONAUR

AVAILABLE IN SOFTCOVER OR HARDCOVER WITH DUST JACKET

WAR BEYOND THE DRAGON PAGODA by *J. J. Snodgrass*—A Personal Narrative of the First Anglo-Burmese War 1824 - 1826.

ALL FOR A SHILLING A DAY by *Donald F. Featherstone*—The story of H.M. 16th, the Queen's Lancers During the first Sikh War 1845-1846.

AT THEM WITH THE BAYONET by *Donald F. Featherstone*—The first Anglo-Sikh War 1845-1846.

A LEONAUR ORIGINAL

THE HERO OF ALIWAL by *James Humphries*—The days when young Harry Smith wore the green jacket of the 95th-Wellington's famous riflemen-campaigning in Spain against Napoleon's French with his beautiful young bride Juana have long gone. Now, Sir Harry Smith is in his fifties approaching the end of a long career. His position in the Cape colony ends with an appointment as Deputy Adjutant-General to the army in India. There he joins the staff of Sir Hugh Gough to experience an Indian battlefield in the Gwalior War of 1843 as the power of the Marathas is finally crushed. Smith has little time for his superior's 'bull at a gate' style of battlefield tactics, but independent command is denied him. Little does he realise that the greatest opportunity of his military life is close at hand.

THE GURKHA WAR by *H. T. Prinsep*—The Anglo-Nepalese Conflict in North East India 1814-1816.

SOUND ADVANCE! by *Joseph Anderson*—Experiences of an officer of HM 50th regiment in Australia, Burma & the Gwalior war.

THE CAMPAIGN OF THE INDUS by *Thomas Holdsworth*—Experiences of a British Officer of the 2nd (Queen's Royal) Regiment in the Campaign to Place Shah Shuja on the Throne of Afghanistan 1838 - 1840.

WITH THE MADRAS EUROPEAN REGIMENT IN BURMA by *John Butler*—The Experiences of an Officer of the Honourable East India Company's Army During the First Anglo-Burmese War 1824 - 1826.

BESIEGED IN LUCKNOW by *Martin Richard Gubbins*—The Experiences of the Defender of 'Gubbins Post' before & during the sige of the residency at Lucknow, Indian Mutiny, 1857.

THE STORY OF THE GUIDES by *G.J. Younghusband*—The Exploits of the famous Indian Army Regiment from the northwest frontier 1847 - 1900.

LEONAUR

ALSO FROM LEONAUR

AVAILABLE IN SOFTCOVER OR HARDCOVER WITH DUST JACKET

SEPOYS, SIEGE & STORM by *Charles John Griffiths*—The Experiences of a young officer of H.M.'s 61st Regiment at Ferozepore, Delhi ridge and at the fall of Delhi during the Indian mutiny 1857.

THE RECOLLECTIONS OF SKINNER OF SKINNER'S HORSE by *James Skinner*—James Skinner and his 'Yellow Boys' Irregular cavalry in the wars of India between the British, Mahratta, Rajput, Mogul, Sikh & Pindarree Forces.

A CAVALRY OFFICER DURING THE SEPOY REVOLT by *A. R. D. Mackenzie*—Experiences with the 3rd Bengal Light Cavalry, the Guides and Sikh Irregular Cavalry from the outbreak to Delhi and Lucknow.

A NORFOLK SOLDIER IN THE FIRST SIKH WAR by *J. W. Baldwin*—Experiences of a private of H.M. 9th Regiment of Foot in the battles for the Punjab, India 1845-6.

TOMMY ATKINS' WAR STORIES Fourteen first hand accounts from the ranks of the British Army during Queen Victoria's Empire Original & True Battle Stories Recollections of the Indian Mutiny With the 49th in the Crimea With the Guards in Egypt The Charge of the Six Hundred With Wolseley in Ashanti Alma, Inkermann and Magdala With the Gunners at Tel-el-Kebir Russian Guns and Indian Rebels Rough Work in the Crimea In the Maori Rising Facing the Zulus From Sebastopol to Lucknow Sent to Save Gordon On the March to Chitral Tommy by Rudyard Kipling.

THE KHAKEE RESSALAH by *Robert Henry Wallace Dunlop*—Service & adventure with the Meerut volunteer horse during the Indian mutiny 1857-1858.

Milton Keynes UK
Ingram Content Group UK Ltd.
UKHW020721060924
1525UKWH00005B/7